Fodor's

Tokyo's 25Best

by Martin Gostelow

Fodor's Travel Publications
New York • Toronto
London • Sydney • Auckland
www.fodors.com

How to Use This Book

KEY TO SYMBOLS

- Map reference to the accompanying fold-out map
- Address
- Telephone number
- Opening/closing times
- Restaurant or café
- Nearest rail station
- Nearest subway (Metro) station
- Nearest bus route
- Nearest riverboat or ferry stop
- Facilities for visitors with disabilities
- Other practical information
- Further information
- Tourist information
- Admission charges: Expensive (over ¥8,000), Moderate (¥3,000–¥8,000), and Inexpensive (¥3,000 or less)
- Major Sight
- Minor Sight
- Walks
- Excursions
- Shops
- Entertainment and Nightlife
- Restaurants

This guide is divided into four sections

- Essential Tokyo: An introduction to the city and tips on making the most of your stay.
- Tokyo by Area: We've broken the city into six areas, and recommended the best sights, shops, entertainment venues, nightlife and restaurants in each one. Suggested walks help you to explore on foot.
- Where to Stay: The best hotels, whether you're looking for luxury, budget or something in between.
- Need to Know: The info you need to make your trip run smoothly, including getting about by public transport, weather tips, emergency phone numbers and useful websites.

Navigation In the Tokyo by Area chapter, we've given each area its own color, which is also used on the locator maps throughout the book and the map on the inside front cover.

Maps The fold-out map accompanying this book is a comprehensive street plan of Tokyo. The grid on this fold-out map is the same as the grid on the locator maps within the book. We've given grid references within the book for each sight and listing. For the Shopping, Entertainment and Nightlife, Restaurants and Hotels listings, the grid references refer to the nearest rail/subway station. From here you will find clear directions on the detailed maps provided near the station exits.

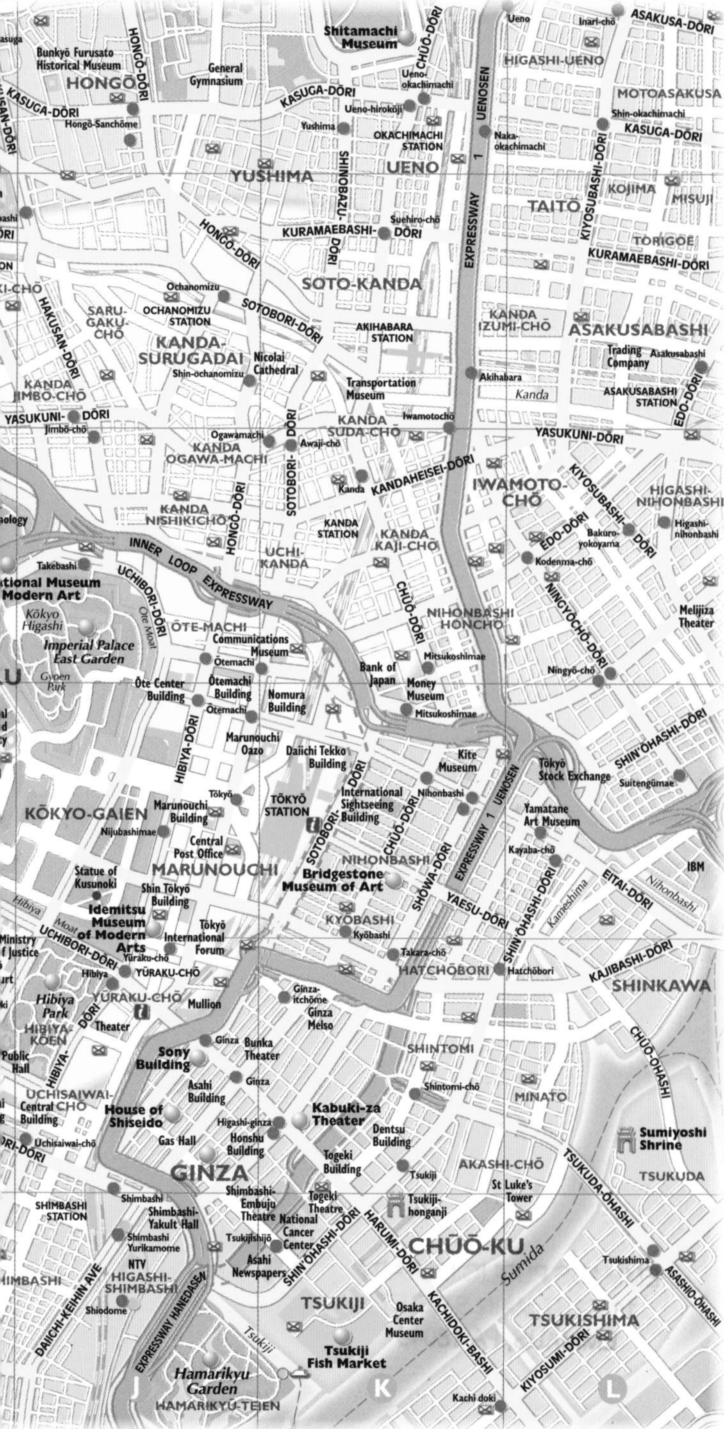

Bunkyō Furusato Historical Museum
HONGŌ
HONGŌ-DŌRI
KASUGA-DŌRI
Hongō-Sanchōme
General Gymnasium
Shitamachi Museum
CHŪŌ-DŌRI
Ueno-okachimachi
Ueno-hirokōji
Yushima
OKACHIMACHI STATION
YUSHIMA
SHINOBAZU-DŌRI
UENO
Suehiro-chō
KURAMAEBASHI-DŌRI
SOTO-KANDA
UENOSEN
EXPRESSWAY 1
Naka-okachimachi
Ueno
Inari-chō
ASAKUSA-DŌRI
HIGASHI-UENO
MOTOASAKUSA
Shin-okachimachi
KASUGA-DŌRI
KIYOSUBASHI-DŌRI
KOJIMA
MISUJI
TAITŌ
TORIGOE
KURAMAEBASHI-DŌRI
HONGŌ-DŌRI
Ochanomizu
OCHANOMIZU STATION
SOTOBORI-DŌRI
SARU-GAKU-CHŌ
HAKUSAN-DŌRI
KANDA-SURUGADAI
Nicolai Cathedral
Shin-ochanomizu
AKIHABARA STATION
Transportation Museum
KANDA IZUMI-CHŌ
ASAKUSABASHI
Trading Company
Asakusabashi
ASAKUSABASHI STATION
Akihabara
Kanda
EDO-DŌRI
KANDA JIMBŌ-CHŌ
YASUKUNI-DŌRI
Jimbō-chō
Ogawamachi
Awaji-chō
KANDA SUDA-CHŌ
Iwamotochō
YASUKUNI-DŌRI
KANDA OGAWA-MACHI
SOTOBORI-DŌRI
Kanda
KANDAHEISEI-DŌRI
IWAMOTO-CHŌ
KIYOSUBASHI-DŌRI
HIGASHI-NIHONBASHI
Higashi-nihonbashi
KANDA NISHIKICHŌ
HONGŌ-DŌRI
KANDA STATION
KANDA KAJI-CHŌ
EDO-DŌRI
Bakuro-yokoyama
UCHI-KANDA
Kodenma-chō
INNER LOOP EXPRESSWAY
Takebashi
National Museum of Modern Art
UCHIBORI-DŌRI
Ote Moat
Kōkyo Higashi
Imperial Palace East Garden
Gyoen Park
ŌTE-MACHI
Communications Museum
Ōtemachi
CHŪŌ-DŌRI
NIHONBASHI HONCHŌ
Mitsukoshimae
NINGYŌCHŌ-DŌRI
Meijiza Theater
Ōte Center Building
Ōtemachi Building
Ōtemachi
Nomura Building
Bank of Japan
Money Museum
Mitsukoshimae
Ningyō-chō
HIBIYA-DŌRI
Marunouchi Oazo
Daiichi Tekko Building
Kite Museum
Tōkyō Stock Exchange
SHIN'ŌHASHI-DŌRI
Suitengūmae
Tōkyō
TŌKYŌ STATION
International Sightseeing Building
Nihonbashi
KŌKYO-GAIEN
Marunouchi Building
Nijubashimae
Central Post Office
SOTOBORI-DŌRI
CHŪŌ-DŌRI
Yamatane Art Museum
Kayaba-chō
MARUNOUCHI
NIHONBASHI
Bridgestone Museum of Art
SHŌWA-DŌRI
SHIN'ŌHASHI-DŌRI
EITAI-DŌRI
IBM
Nihonbashi
Kameshima
YAESU-DŌRI
Statue of Kusunoki
Shin Tōkyō Building
Idemitsu Museum of Modern Arts
Tōkyō International Forum
Hibiya
Moat
KYŌBASHI
Kyōbashi
Ministry of Justice
UCHIBORI-DŌRI
Yūraku-chō
Takara-chō
Hibiya
YŪRAKU-CHŌ
HATCHŌBORI
Hatchōbori
KAJIBASHI-DŌRI
SHINKAWA
Hibiya Park
HIBIYA-KŌEN
HIBIYA-DŌRI
Theater
Mullion
Ginza-itchōme
Ginza Melso
CHŪŌ-ŌHASHI
Public Hall
Ginza
Sony Building
Bunka Theater
SHINTOMI
Asahi Building
Ginza
Shintomi-chō
MINATO
UCHISAIWAI-CHŌ
Central Building
House of Shiseido
Higashi-ginza
Kabuki-za Theater
Dentsu Building
Sumiyoshi Shrine
Uchisaiwai-chō
Gas Hall
Honshu Building
Togeki Building
Tsukiji
AKASHI-CHŌ
TSUKUDA
GINZA
St Luke's Tower
Shimbashi
SHIMBASHI STATION
Shimbashi-Embuju Theatre
Togeki Theatre
Tsukiji-honganji
Shimbashi-Yakult Hall
National Cancer Center
HARUMI-DŌRI
TSUKUDA-ŌHASHI
Shimbashi Yurikamome
Tsukijishijō
SHIN'ŌHASHI-DŌRI
CHŪŌ-KU
Sumida
Tsukishima
ASASHIO-ŌHASHI
NTV
HIGASHI-SHIMBASHI
Asahi Newspapers
DAIICHI-KEIHIN AVE
EXPRESSWAY HANEDASEN
Shiodome
TSUKIJI
Osaka Center Museum
KACHIDOKI-BASHI
TSUKISHIMA
KIYOSUMI-DŌRI
Tsukiji
Tsukiji Fish Market
Hamarikyu Garden
HAMARIKYŪ-TEIEN
Kachi doki
J
K
L

Contents

ESSENTIAL TOKYO 4–18

Introducing Tokyo 4–5
A Short Stay in Tokyo 6–7
Top 25 8–9
Shopping 10–11
Shopping by Theme 12
Tokyo by Night 13
Eating Out 14
Restaurants by Cuisine 15
If You Like... 16–18

TOKYO BY AREA 19–106

SHIBUYA-KU AND SHINJUKU-KU 20–38

Area Map 22–23
Sights 24–33
Walk 34
Shopping 35
Entertainment and Nightlife 36
Restaurants 37–38

AROUND ROPPONGI 39–50

Area Map 40-41
Sights 42-46
Shopping 47
Entertainment and Nightlife 48
Restaurants 49–50

CHIYODA-KU 51–64

Area Map 52–53
Sights 54–60
Walk 61
Shopping 62
Entertainment and Nightlife 63
Restaurants 64

AROUND GINZA 65–82

Area Map 66–67
Sights 68–76
Walk 77
Shopping 78
Entertainment and Nightlife 79–80
Restaurants 81–82

UENO 83–96

Area Map 84–85
Sights 86–93
Walk 94
Shopping 95
Entertainment and Nightlife 95
Restaurants 96

FARTHER AFIELD 97–106

Area Map 98–99
Sights 100–105
Excursions 106

WHERE TO STAY 107–112

Introduction 108
Budget Hotels 109
Mid-Range Hotels 110–111
Luxury Hotels 112

NEED TO KNOW 113–125

Planning Ahead 114–115
Getting There 116–117
Getting Around 118–119
Essential Facts 120–122
Language 123
Timeline 124–125

Introducing Tokyo

While Japan's capital and the country's largest city may appear daunting for the first-time visitor, it has a super-efficient transportation system and helpful people, which will make your sightseeing endeavors very easy and well worth the effort.

This modern metropolis, with its conglomeration of retail, entertainment, business and industrial districts and its beautiful shrines, temples and gardens, is made up of unique self-contained districts. Each one–just minutes away from the next on the subway system–is like a separate town or village.

Perhaps start in glitzy Ginza district, home to the wealthy, or vibrant Harajuku, where young people strut their stuff at the outdoor cafés set on chic Omotesando-dori, regarded as Tokyo's Champs-Élysées.

Then you can flit from working-class Ueno with its budget shopping and cultural institutions, in the north, to up-and-coming Ikebukuro, set between Ueno and bustling Shinjuku. Or head for Odaiba, the shopping and entertainment complex to the south of the city, and the stunning Roppongi Hills complex where the latest urban design forms a backdrop for brand-name shops.

After dark, elaborate neon signs transform parts of Tokyo. Flashing signs and glowing lanterns in 100,000 restaurants and drinking dens beckon. In contrast, on weekends, you'll find parents congregating in parks and gardens with their much-adored children.

Few historic buildings remain, as the massive 1923 earthquake and World War II bombing destroyed much of the city. Yet charming corners turn up in unexpected places. Local shrines nestle in the shadow of expressways, art collections can be found in office towers, and one of the world's great bonsai collections turns up in a suburban office building.

Facts + Figures

- **There are more restaurants per capita in Tokyo than anywhere else in the world.**
- **Life expectancy is age 84 for women and age 77 for men (among the world's highest).**
- **There are over 5 million motor vehicles in the city.**

NEIGHBORHOODS

Tokyo and its suburbs, home to around 12 million people, sprawl across the Kanto Plain on Japan's largest island, Honshu. The metropolitan area is divided into 23 wards (*ku*)–of which most visitors see only five or six around central Tokyo. Within these wards are districts that, for the purposes of this book, are defined according to their major attractions.

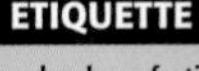

ETIQUETTE

The intricate local rules of etiquette do not apply to visitors to Japan. However, to please your hosts, always take your shoes off when entering a house or room with straw matting. And remember that a slight bow is good form after you buy something in a shop or when meeting people.

THE OFFICE LADY

A woman is traditionally not expected to have a career. To fill in the years until she gets married, she might work as an *oeru* (office lady or OL–pronounced "o-eru"). While men take the "real" jobs, the *oeru* shuffles paper, pours tea and looks pretty. But she exacts a sort of revenge: Unlike the young salaryman, who has to spend his spare money partying with colleagues, the *oeru* can save her money to take foreign holidays. Western pressures and influences are encouraging younger Japanese women to be much more assertive and to enjoy life.

A Short Stay in Tokyo

DAY 1

Morning Have an early breakfast at **Tsukiji Fish Market** (▷ 75) after a look at the hustle and bustle of the aftermath of the fish auctions and the many market stalls.

Mid-morning Hop on the subway and head for nearby **Ginza** (▷ 68), walking the wide Harumi-dori where specialty shops and department stores abound. It's less crowded than in the afternoon and you can always come back in the evening for the neon spectacular. Drop in and check out the latest technology at the **Sony Building** (▷ 73).

Lunch Pick up a *bento* box in the basement food halls of one of the department stores (be sure to taste the free samples that are always on offer) and head for the delightful Western-style **Hibiya Park** (▷ 56) for lunch on the park benches with the office workers.

Afternoon Head for Asakusa via the subway for a glimpse of old Japan and the bustling stalls of Nakamise-dori that make up the approach to the Asakusa Kannon Temple (▷ 86) with its huge bell and nearby five-story pagoda.

Dinner From here you can walk back to the Ginza district for a meal at any one of the many small restaurants to be found in the back streets and laneways off the main thoroughfares.

Evening Marvel at the street scenes highlighted by neon lights and huge-screen video displays that use the latest technology to display eye-catching advertising. You could take in a one-act play at the famous old **Kabuki-za Theater** (▷ 72).

DAY 2

Morning A morning visit to the carefully tended **Imperial Palace East Garden** (▷ 54) with its huge stone walls gives you a glimpse of Tokyo's royal past. Something is always blooming here and even in winter the gardens present quite a dramatic look.

Mid-morning Take the subway to **Harajuku** (▷ 24) from where you can take a short walk through the towering *torii* (gate) to the stunning **Meiji Jingu Shrine** (▷ 25) set in its forested precinct.

Lunch Head back on foot to Harajuku station with its myriad nearby dining options, although a delicious sushi lunch can be had at **Kakiya Sushi** (▷ 38).

Afternoon Explore the festive **Takeshita-dori street market shops** (▷ 24) before taking a stroll down the wide **Omotesando-dori** (▷ 24) where Parisian-style outdoor cafés make the perfect coffee stop.

Mid-afternoon Visit the small **Ota Memorial Museum of Art** (▷ 31) with its stunning collection of *ukiyo-e* (woodblock) prints. Take the subway to **Roppongi Hills** (▷ 42) with its fine shopping and dining complex.

Dinner There are any number of restaurants around the streets but you could choose to dine with the locals on tatami mats at **Hassan** (▷ 50).

Evening There are plenty of good nightspots around Roppongi, but try **Mogambo** (▷ 48) if you like hip music and a view of the expat drinking scene.

Top 25

Asakusa Kannon Temple ▷ **86–87** Tokyo's oldest temple, dedicated to Kannon, goddess of mercy.

Edo-Tokyo Museum ▷ **88** Scenes from Tokyo's cultural and commercial past in a futuristic building.

Ginza ▷ **68–69** The most famous shopping and entertainment district in the whole of Japan.

Yebisu Garden Place ▷ **45** Shops, museums and restaurants on the site of a former brewery.

Yasukuni Shrine ▷ **59** A national monument dedicated to those who died defending the Japanese empire.

Tsukiji Fish Market ▷ **75** Even though the early-morning tuna auctions are off limits, there are 1,200 stalls to visit instead.

Tokyo Tower ▷ **74** This Eiffel Tower-like structure stands at 1,092ft (333m).

Tokyo National Museum ▷ **90–91** The whole history of Japan and Japanese art is covered here.

Tokyo Disney Resort ▷ **103** The DisneySea Park is the world's first Disney Park to be inspired by the legends of the sea.

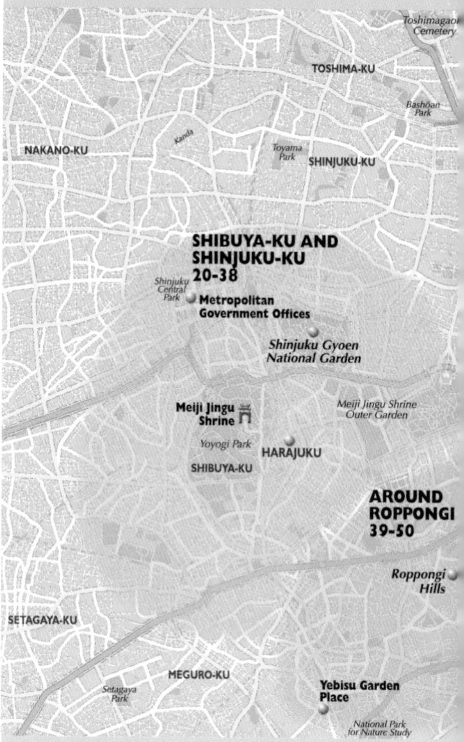

Toshimagaoka Cemetery
TOSHIMA-KU
Bashōan Park
NAKANO-KU
Kanda
Toyama Park
SHINJUKU-KU
SHIBUYA-KU AND SHINJUKU-KU 20-38
Shinjuku Central Park
Metropolitan Government Offices
Shinjuku Gyoen National Garden
Meiji Jingu Shrine
Meiji Jingu Shrine Outer Garden
Yoyogi Park
HARAJUKU
SHIBUYA-KU
AROUND ROPPONGI 39-50
Roppongi Hills
SETAGAYA-KU
MEGURO-KU
Setagaya Park
Yebisu Garden Place
National Park for Nature Study

Sony Building ▷ **73** New products and developments are on display in the Sony showrooms.

Shinjuku Gyoen National Garden ▷ **28–29** A huge national park with beautifully landscaped gardens.

Sengakuji Temple ▷ **44** The 47 *ronin* buried in this temple are revered as examples of truly loyal men.

These pages are a quick guide to the Top 25, which are described in more detail later. Here they are listed alphabetically, and the tinted background shows which area they are in.

Hamarikyu Garden and River Cruise ▷ 70–71 Go on a cruise upriver from this peaceful garden.

Harajuku ▷ 24 Both street markets and boutiques can be found in this lively neighborhood.

Hibiya Park ▷ 56 Escape from the bustle of the city to the tranquillity of Tokyo's first public park.

Imperial Palace East Garden ▷ 54–55 A welcome oasis in the noise and fumes of downtown Tokyo.

Kabuki-za Theater ▷ 72 A unique cultural experience, one that should not be missed.

Meiji Jingu Shrine ▷ 25 A shrine dedicated to Emperor Meiji and his wife.

Metropolitan Government Offices ▷ 26–27 A vast, expensive show of architectural bravura.

National Diet Building ▷ 57 This opulent building houses Japan's national legislature.

National Museum of Modern Art ▷ 58 The best of Japanese painting.

National Museum of Western Art ▷ 89 Don't miss the European masters on display here.

Roppongi Hills ▷ 42–43 Japan's largest urban redevelopment complex includes a 54-story tower.

Rikugien Garden ▷ 102 The lovely "six-poem garden" was laid out in the 17th century.

Odaiba ▷ 100–101 Shopping, entertainment and exhibition facilities, and a beach on reclaimed land.

Shopping

Shop early, shop often! Tokyo is a shopper's paradise and for the locals it is serious business. The place to begin shopping in Tokyo is at the large department stores. Here you'll find floors of merchandise, all of which is beautifully designed and in extreme good taste. Look out especially for fashion goods, homewares, including exquisite ceramics, lacquerware and soft furnishings, and arts and crafts such as miniature dolls. These stores are located in most precincts and shopping areas.

Electronics

Since the Japanese invented consumer electronics, the products that we can no longer live without, Tokyo is a good place to look for (or at) the latest electronic gadgetry. You might begin at one of the many technology show-rooms, such as the Sony Building (▷ 73) in Ginza.

Shopping Rules

While it may be a case of look but don't buy in some of Ginza's chic shops, such as Mikimoto (▷ 78), many specialty shops, especially in the back streets, have reasonably priced clothing, including kimonos, lovely paper products, traditional fans and way-out designer goods. In fact, a good rule for Tokyo shopping, since addresses are often impossible to find, is to wander the back-streets of Shinjuku, Shibuya, Ginza, Ikebukuro and Asakusa in search of your own treasures. Every product, no matter how utilitarian, is wrapped or boxed with great care.

Amusing sumo wrestling souvenirs, traditional gifts and the latest digital cameras–it's all here in Tokyo

COMIC CULT

Perhaps the weirdest craze in Japan is the nation's obsession with manga, the comic books of all genres that rail commuters engross themselves in. This has led to anime, or animation, the film equivalent that manifests itself in a variety of television and film products. There are plenty of anime shops around Akihabara (▷ 62).

Street Markets

Street markets such as those found near Ueno station are good places to get a general idea of Japanese merchandise. Local shoppers will be looking for something new to wear or choosing dinner from the huge array of seafood, vegetables, dried foods and prepared meals. The Japanese love of packaging makes prepared food items a very tempting retail adventure. The variety, freshness and quality of what's on offer defies belief; from sushi to tempura, noodle meals (*soba* and *udon*) to luscious, if expensive *unagi* (eel) dishes.

Traditional Wares

The best flea markets (▷ 12) are a good place to shop for antiques, although you're unlikely to find bargains. They are, however, great places to learn about Japanese wares, art, old kimonos and assorted bric-a-brac and to purchase something from the old days as a memento.

Shopping Streets

While some of Tokyo's classiest shops are found in the main streets of Ginza, be sure to check out the high fashion shops on Omotesando-dori and the funky outlets in nearby Takeshita-dori (▷ below). Budget shoppers and adventurous foodies should head to Ueno for the bustling Ameyoko Arcade, an open-air pedestrian-friendly bazaar.

TAKESHITA-DORI

Takeshita-dori is a paradigm of youth culture. There is nowhere quite like this busy shopping street beginning just opposite Harajuku station near the famed Omotesando-dori. The narrow lane is crammed with shops selling fashion to Japanese teenagers—arguably the world's most avid consumers (from imported brand-name labels to obscure local fashion labels that are found nowhere else in the world). In the streets around here on weekends the young dress in the most outlandish gear, so have your camera ready.

Shopping by Theme

Whether you're looking for a department store, a quirky boutique, or something inbetween, you'll find it all in Tokyo. On this page shops are listed by theme. For a more detailed write-up, see the individual listings in Tokyo by Area.

ANTIQUES AND HANDICRAFTS

Antiques Hasebe-Ya (▷ 47)
Aoyama Book Center (▷ 47)
Aoyama Oval Plaza (▷ 35)
Bingo Ya (▷ 35)
Fuji-Torii (▷ 35)
International Arcade (▷ 78)
Kurofune Antiques (▷ 47)
Minami-Aoyama (▷ 47)
Oriental Bazaar (▷ 35)
Roppongi Antique Bazaar (▷ 47)
Washikobo (▷ 47)

BOOKS

Isseido (▷ 62)
Kanda-Jimbocho (▷ 62)
Kinokuniya (▷ 35)
Maruzen (▷ 78)
Ohya-Shobo (▷ 62)

BUDGET/ DISCOUNT STORES

Daiso Harajuku (▷ 35)
Don Quijote (▷ 47)

CAMERAS/JEWELRY

BIC Camera (▷ 62)
Mikimoto (▷ 78)
Tasaki Pearl Gallery (▷ 47)

CERAMICS

Kisso (▷ 47)
Koransha (▷ 78)

CHILDREN/TEENS

Kiddyland (▷ 35)
Tokyo Anime Center (▷ 62)

DEPARTMENT STORES

Isetan (▷ 35)
Matsuya (▷ 78)
Mitsukoshi (▷ 78)
Seibu (▷ 35)
Takashimaya (▷ 78)
Tokyu (▷ 35)
Tokyu Hands (▷ 35)

ELECTRICAL/ ELECTRONIC GOODS

Akihabara (▷ 62)
HMV (▷ 35)
Ishimaru Denki (▷ 62)
Laox (▷ 62)
Minami Musen (▷ 62)
Yamagiwa (▷ 62)
Yodobashi-Akiba (▷ 62)

FLEA MARKETS/ MARKETS

Ameyoko Market (▷ 95)
Nogi Shrine Flea Market (▷ 47)
Togo Shrine (▷ 35)
Tsukiji Fish Market (▷ 75)

INTERIOR DECORATION

Axis (▷ 47)

SHOPPING MALLS AND STREETS

Kappabashi (▷ 95)
LaForêt (▷ 35)
Nakamise-dori (▷ 95)
Odaiba (▷ 100)
Roppongi Hills (▷ 42)
Shiodome (▷ 78)
Yebisu Garden Place (▷ 45)

STATIONERY

Ito-Ya (▷ 78)
Kyukyodo (▷ 78)
Ginza-Yurakucho (▷ 78)

Tokyo by Night

Buzzing street life, great nighttime views and cultural entertainment are all on offer after dark

Tokyo really comes to life at night. Restaurants offering traditional meals, little eating places where cuisine triumphs over the surroundings, late-opening nightclubs where fusion music is taken to new extremes and bars filled with karaoke-singing revelers are all part of the Tokyo experience.

Out on the Town

Western visitors to Tokyo who want a night on the town generally head to the Roppongi area, whose dance clubs, bars and pubs attract local expats (*gaijin*) and Japanese alike and where the action continues until the small hours. Shibuya attracts a younger crowd, and there are any number of live music venues—best discovered by checking a website such as www.tokyoessentials.com (▷ 115).

Night Tours

If you are a bit tentative about venturing out at night, consider a night tour. These generally combine dinner with a show and a drive-through of Ginza or Akasaka, with their dramatic displays of neon signage. You have a choice of menus, perhaps *sukiyaki* (meat simmered in a hot skillet), *kushiage* (deep-fried morsels on sticks) or steak; the show is usually kabuki theater or traditional geisha entertainment of music, song and conversation although true geishas don't speak English. Also popular are dinner cruises on Tokyo Bay that give you some great views of the Rainbow suspension bridge over the bay, Fuji Television building and Tokyo Disney Resort by night.

DRINK PRICES

Drinks at some bars range from very expensive (up to ¥10,000 at a hostess bar) to inexpensive or moderate, ¥500 at a *aka-chochin* or *nomiya*, the small red lantern bars that are everywhere. In between are pub-like *yakitori-ya*, Japanese-style places where you can get food, beer and sake.

Eating Out

For Tokyoites, dining out is an integral part of everyday life, and many people eat more often in restaurants than they do at home, where space is mostly too limited for socializing. As a result, there is an enormous variety of eateries in Tokyo, with something to suit every taste and pocket.

Customs

Once seated in a restaurant, you will be given *oshibori*, *ohashi* and *ocha*. *Oshibori* are small, napkin-size damp cloths, heated in cold weather and cold in hot weather. Use them to wipe your hands and face, and then as napkins during the meal. *Ohashi* are chopsticks. *Ocha*, or green tea, is part of Japanese life. It is the common offering in restaurants, given out free when you arrive and at the end of the meal.

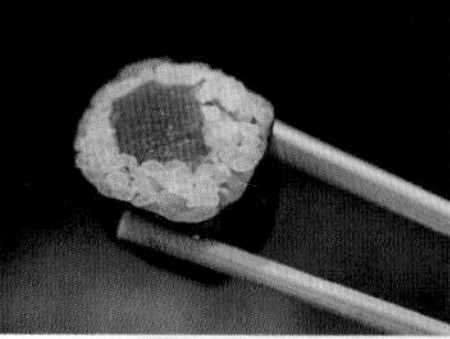

Places to Eat

Robatayaki restaurants are cheerful, noisy places where varied foods are cooked on an open grill amid clouds of smoke. A *ryori-ya* or *shokudo* is a mixed-menu restaurant: Plastic replicas in the window show the choices and prices. *Chuka ryori-ya* are basic Chinese restaurants, often visited by Japanese families for a cheap meal, serving such staples as fried rice and noodle dishes. *Ramen-ya* and *soba-ya* serve inexpensive bowls of noodles in a soup or with a topping. A *kissaten* is a coffeehouse serving light snacks and sweet pastries—the coffee may be expensive but you can sit as long as you like. For a moderately priced breakfast of toast, coffee, a boiled egg and small salad, ask for *moningu sabisu* ("morning service").

ECONOMY

- Avoid restaurants that only provide Western food as they tend to be more expensive. Likewise, Western foods such as bread, cake and cheese are more costly than traditional Japanese foods.
- The most expensive restaurants do not display prices.
- Alcohol is expensive in bars and clubs.

Sidewalk or fine dining, the choice is yours—and take a look at what's on offer in the local bakeries, too

Restaurants by Cuisine

There are restaurants to suit all tastes and budgets in Tokyo. On this page they are listed by cuisine. For a more detailed description of each restaurant, see Tokyo by Area.

JAPANESE

Asahi Zushi (▷ 37)
Bikkuri Sushi (▷ 49)
Daidaiya (▷ 81)
Denpachi (▷ 64)
Edogin (▷ 81)
Fukuzushi (▷ 49)
Futaba (▷ 96)
Ganko (▷ 81)
Hachiuta (▷ 37)
Hassan (▷ 50)
Irimoya (▷ 81)
Izu'ei (▷ 96)
Kakiya Sushi (▷ 38)
Kuremutsu (▷ 96)
Kyubei (▷ 81)
Maimon (▷ 38)
Maisen (▷ 38)
Munakata (▷ 81)
Myoko (▷ 38)
Nakasei (▷ 96)
Namiki Yabu Soba (▷ 96)
Negishi (▷ 38)
Nobu Tokyo (▷ 50)
Robata (▷ 64)
Sansada (▷ 96)
Shabuzen (▷ 50)
Sushi Dai (▷ 82)
Takara (▷ 82)
Takeno (▷ 82)
Tarafuku (▷ 82)
Ten Ichi (▷ 82)
Tsuki No Shizuku (▷ 64)
Tsunahachi (▷ 38)
Wasai Ginza (▷ 82)
Yabu Soba (▷ 64)
Yoshinari (▷ 82)

THAI

Chang-Plai (▷ 37)
Chiang Mai (▷ 81)
Coriander (▷ 49)
Mai-Thai (▷ 38)
The Siam (▷ 82)

INDIAN

Ajanta (▷ 64)
Bindi (▷ 49)
Kenbokke (▷ 50)
Mantra (▷ 96)
Moti (▷ 50)
Tandoor (▷ 38)

OTHER ASIAN

Asena (▷ 49)
Athara Petara (▷ 49)
Bengawan Solo (▷ 49)
Bougainvillea (▷ 37)
Monsoon (▷ 81)
Palette (▷ 38)

ITALIAN

Il Boccalone (▷ 37)
La Bohème (▷ 37)
Capricciosa (▷ 49)
Carmine Edochiano (▷ 37)
Lintaro (▷ 81)
Sicilia (▷ 50)
La Verde (▷ 50)

OTHER WESTERN

Andersen (▷ 49)
Anna Miller's (▷ 49)
Bistro de Maido (▷ 37)
El Castellano (▷ 37)
Las Chicas (▷ 37)
Club NYX (▷ 64)
Dole Fruit Café (▷ 37)
Good Honest Grub (▷ 37)
Johnny Rockets (▷ 50)
Kua'Aina (▷ 50)
News Deli (▷ 50)
Omiya (▷ 96)
Rosita (▷ 38)
Rosso e Nero (▷ 64)
Samovar (▷ 38)
T.G.I. Friday's (▷ 82)
Tokyo Joe's (▷ 64)
Ueno Seiyoken Grill (▷ 96)

If You Like...

However you'd like to spend your time in Tokyo, these top suggestions should help you tailor your ideal visit. Each sight or listing has a fuller write-up in Tokyo by Area.

SAMPLING LOCAL CUISINE

Visit the food halls of department stores (▷ 12), located in the store basements–the best place to sample local foods.

Eat at Robata, an old-style wooden restaurant (▷ 64), which features traditional country cuisine including tofu and pork dishes.

OUTDOOR DINING

Walk down elegant Omotesando-dori (▷ 24) and have a snack and coffee at one of the many Parisian-style outdoor cafés.

Head for the Kudan Kaikan Beer Garden (▷ 63), popular from May to September for its rooftop dining and drinking scene.

Raw fish sushi (top) and life on busy Omotesando-dori (above)

ELECTRONIC GOODS

Explore Akihabara (▷ 62) with its myriad electronics shops to compare models and prices on cameras, iPods, and other consumer electronics.

Try out the products at the Sony Building (▷ 73), which has six floors packed with the latest electronic gizmos.

SHOPPING FOR BRAND-NAME CLOTHES

The big department stores and specialty shops in the Ginza-Yurakucho district (▷ 78) have every brand name on offer.

At Odaiba (▷ 100) in the Tokyo Bay area, you'll find VenusFort, a theme shopping mall decorated in classical style.

Looking for a laptop (above right) and a spot of designer shopping (right)

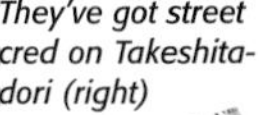
They've got street cred on Takeshita-dori (right)

LEARNING ABOUT LOCAL CULTURE

Funky Takeshita-dori (▷ 24) is the best place to view Tokyo's teen dress-up scene as young people parade in their outlandish costumes.

Attend a performance at the Kabuki-za Theater (▷ 72) to see actors perform the scenes from this ancient operatic art form.

GOING OUT ON THE TOWN

Mix with the locals at the Beer Station (▷ 36), either at a table or at the counter from where you can order plates of tasty snacks.

See international musicians perform a variety of acts at Blue Note Tokyo (▷ 48) and enjoy cocktails and delicious food.

STAYING AT BUDGET HOTELS

Experience traditional lodgings at Tokyo's most popular ryokan, Sawanoya Ryokan (▷ 109), where the hosts are a font of local information.

Budget Western-style accommodations are available at the Asia Center of Japan (▷ 109), but be sure to make a booking well in advance.

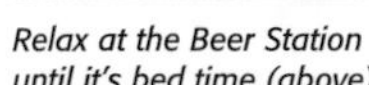
Relax at the Beer Station until it's bed time (above)

ENTERTAINING THE KIDS

The Tokyo Anime Center (▷ 63) has regular screenings of popular anime and previews of the latest animation trends.

Nothing beats the traditional and popular attractions at Tokyo Disney Resort (▷ 103), where the kids are transported to a world of fun.

These Japanese kids are traveling in style (left)

A GIRLS' NIGHT OUT

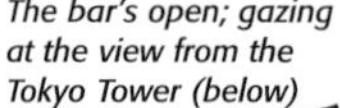

The bar's open; gazing at the view from the Tokyo Tower (below)

Techno and Progressive House fans should head for Womb (▷ 36) for good music, a range of drinks and tasty eats.

Twenty Eight (▷ 79), one of Tokyo's most stylish bars, presents jazz singers, cocktails and classic Tokyo city light views.

THE BEST VIEWS IN TOWN

Tokyo City View (▷ 42) atop the Roppongi Hills complex offers full window views of Tokyo and surrounds in a relaxed setting.

The retro-style Tokyo Tower (▷ 74), although not the tallest vantage point in the city, offers fine inner-city views and various exhibits.

CUTTING-EDGE ARCHITECTURE

Towering urban design at Roppongi Hills (above)

Futuristic urban design with public artworks is a feature of the 11-acre (4.5ha) Roppongi Hills shopping complex and entertainment mall (▷ 42).

See the exhibits and admire the architecture at the Tokyo Metropolitan Museum of Photography (▷ 46) and the adjacent Yebisu Garden Place (▷ 45).

PARKS AND GARDENS

A stroll in Shinjuku Gyoen National Garden (▷ 28) reveals the care and fine garden design that the Japanese lavish on their public green spaces.

Take a guided tour of the Imperial Palace East Garden (▷ 54) and admire the ponds, pathways, plants and towering walls.

People enjoying the beautiful flower displays in the Imperial Palace East Garden (right)

Tokyo by Area

SHIBUYA-KU AND SHINJUKU-KU

Sights	24–33
Walk	34
Shopping	35
Entertainment and Nightlife	36
Restaurants	37–38

AROUND ROPPONGI

Sights	42–46
Shopping	47
Entertainment and Nightlife	48
Restaurants	49–50

CHIYODA-KU

Sights	54–60
Walk	61
Shopping	62
Entertainment and Nightlife	63
Restaurants	64

AROUND GINZA

Sights	68–76
Walk	77
Shopping	78
Entertainment and Nightlife	79–80
Restaurants	81–82

UENO

Sights	86–93
Walk	94
Shopping	95
Entertainment and Nightlife	95
Restaurants	96

FARTHER AFIELD

Sights	100–105
Excursions	106

Shibuya-ku and Shinjuku-ku

Shibuya-ku contrasts the serenity of the Meiji Jingu Shrine with its funky nearby retail and commercial environs in vibrant Harajuku, while bustling Shinjuku-ku has large green spaces, towering office buildings and Japan's busiest rail station.

Sights	**24–33**
Walk	**34**
Shopping	**35**
Entertainment and Nightlife	**36**
Restaurants	**37–38**

Top 25 TOP 25

Harajuku ▷ **24**
Meiji Jingu Shrine ▷ **25**
Metropolitan Government Offices ▷ **26**
Shinjuku Gyoen National Garden ▷ **28**

3
OTAKIBASHI-DŌRI
SEIBU-SHINJUKU
KABUKI-CHŌ
Shinjuku Koma Theater
Hanazono Shrine
Mitsui Building
OME-KAIDŌ
Nishi-shinjuku
Shinjuku-nishiguchi
Shinjuku Square Tower
Nomura Building
Seiji Togo Memorial Art Museum
NISHI-SHINJUKU
Studio Alta
Green Tower Building
Mitsui Building
KITA-DŌRI
Shinjuku Tower Building
My City
Shinjuku sanchōme
4
Nishi-shinjuku-gochome
HŌNAN-DŌRI
Sumitomo Tower
HIGASHI-DŌRI
Center Building
Shinjuku Central Park
Tochōmae
GIJIDO-DŌRI
Keio Plaza Hotel
Shinjuku Station
MEIJI-DŌRI
Metropolitan Government Offices
Shinjuku
Tōei-Kaik Theat
HŌNAN-DŌRI
NS Building
KŌSHŪ-KAIDŌ
Maynds Tower
Takashimaya Times Square Shopping Complex
YAMATE-DŌRI
NTT Shinjuku Building
MINAMI-SHINJUKU
YOYOGI STATION
HON-MACHI
Tokyo Opera City
NTT Intercommunication Center
YOYOGI
Yoyogi
New National Theater Tokyō
5
Japanese Sword Museum
SUIDŌ-DŌRI
Hatsudai
EXPRESSWAY
Treasure House
EXPRESSWAY 4 SHINJUKUSEN
SANGŪBASHI
Meiji-jingū
Meiji-jingu Kaikan Hall
Hatagaya
Sports Center
HATSUDAI
YAMATE-DŌRI
Olympic Memorial Youth Center
Meiji Jingu Shrine
Shrine Office
YOYOGI-KAMIZONO-CHŌ
NISHIHARA
HARAJUK
6
Yoyogi Park
HARAJUKU STATION
Togo Shrine
SHIBUYA-KU
YOYOGI-UEHARA
Ota Memorial Museum of Art
YOYOGIHACHIMAN
ŌYAMA-CHŌ
Yoyogi-Uehara
Yoyogikōenmae
Meijijingūmae
INOKASHIRA-DŌRI
INOKSHIRA-DŌRI
Yogogi Sports Center
Kishi Memorial Gymnasium
NHK Hall
UEHARA
TOMIGAYA
JIN'NAN
NHK Broadcasting Center
BUNKAMURA-DŌRI
INOKASHIRA-DŌRI
KŌEN-DŌRI
Tepco Electric Energy Museum
Shibuya Public Hall
National Childrens Center
Museum of Modern Japanese Literature
7
UDAGAWA-CHŌ
Nihon Mingeikan
METRO-DŌRI
KOMABA
SHŌTŌ
Art Museum
DŌGENZAKA
Shibuya
SHIBUY
Shōtō Museum of Art
SHIBUYA STATION
KOMABA-TODAIMAE
DŌGENZAKA
EXPRESSWAY 3 SHIBUYASE
NANPEI-DAIMACHI
8
0 250 m
0 250 yds
ŌHASHI
HACHIMAN-DŌRI
KYŪ-YAMATE-DŌRI
HACHIYAMA-CHŌ
B
C
AOBADAI
SARUGAKU-CHŌ
D

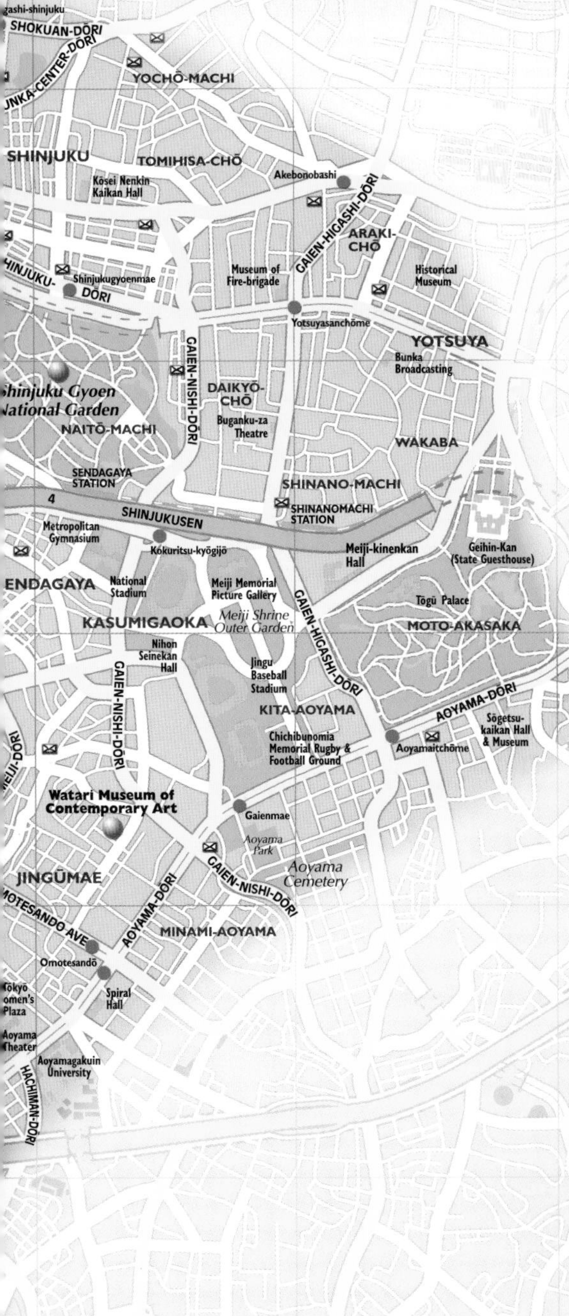

SHOKUAN-DŌRI
YOCHŌ-MACHI
SHINJUKU
TOMIHISA-CHŌ
Kosei Nenkin Kaikan Hall
Akebonobashi
GAIEN-HIGASHI-DŌRI
ARAKI-CHŌ
Museum of Fire-brigade
Historical Museum
Shinjukugyoenmae
DŌRI
Yotsuyasanchōme
YOTSUYA
Bunka Broadcasting
GAIEN-NISHI-DŌRI
DAIKYŌ-CHŌ
Buganku-za Theatre
NAITŌ-MACHI
WAKABA
SENDAGAYA STATION
SHINANO-MACHI
SHINANOMACHI STATION
SHINJUKUSEN
Metropolitan Gymnasium
Kokuritsu-kyōgijō
Meiji-kinenkan Hall
Geihin-Kan (State Guesthouse)
National Stadium
Meiji Memorial Picture Gallery
Tōgū Palace
KASUMIGAOKA
Meiji Shrine Outer Garden
MOTO-AKASAKA
Nihon Seinekan Hall
Jingu Baseball Stadium
KITA-AOYAMA
AOYAMA-DŌRI
Sōgetsu-kaikan Hall & Museum
Chichibunomia Memorial Rugby & Football Ground
Aoyamaitchōme
Watari Museum of Contemporary Art
Gaienmae
Aoyama Park
Aoyama Cemetery
JINGŪMAE
GAIEN-NISHI-DŌRI
MINAMI-AOYAMA
Omotesandō
Spiral Hall
Aoyamagakuin University
HACHIMAN-DŌRI
E
F

Harajuku

Youngsters dress to be admired (left); there's bags of fashion along Takeshita-dori (right)

THE BASICS

- D6
- Harajuku, Shibuya-ku
- A wide choice
- Meijijingu-mae
- Harajuku
- Few
- Free

HIGHLIGHTS

- Takeshita-dori street market
- Omotesando-dori shops
- Ota Memorial Museum of Art's woodblock prints (▷ 31)
- Togo Shrine
- Bi-monthly flea markets
- Yoyogi Park, gardens
- Sports center
- NHK Broadcasting Center tours (▷ 30)
- Teen fashion scene

TIP

- Visit on a weekend, when Tokyo's teens gather around the station to show off their extreme fashions.

The street scene in this neighborhood is a bizarre parade of the young and would-be young in miniskirts and platform shoes, even in winter. Hair is bleached blond or dyed a bright, shocking color.

East of the station Across the street from Harajuku station, Takeshita-dori is an alley lined with stalls selling tinted glasses, music tapes, fast food, coffee and clothing at prices that are bargains, at least by Tokyo standards. Running parallel is the tree-lined Omotesando-dori, with its elegant, expensive boutiques. The nearby Ota Memorial Museum of Art (▷ 31) houses a superb collection of woodblock prints. One of the city's best antiques and flea markets, held on the first and fourth Sunday of each month, is just to the north, off Meiji-dori, near the Togo Shrine (▷ 33). The shrine honors Admiral Togo who was the architect of the Japanese navy that defeated the Russian fleet in 1905.

Yoyogi Park The green space west of Harajuku subway station, next to the grounds of Meiji Jingu Shrine, has been both a US base and home to the 1964 Olympic Games. One of Tokyo's largest city parks, with expansive lawns, pretty ponds and forested areas, the park is popular with joggers, picnickers and cyclists, and as as a gathering place for people to play music and practice martial arts. There are some cherry trees for spring viewing and a ginko tree forest, which turns to golden foliage in the fall.

The Meiji Jingu Shrine is an important site for followers of the Shinto religion in Japan

Meiji Jingu Shrine

Walk through the woods to the national focus of the Shinto religion. Here, people mark important stages of their lives. Babies are brought for their first temple visit and newlyweds come to have marriages blessed.

The shrine The reign of Emperor Meiji (1868–1912) saw Japan transformed from a medieval to a modern state. The shrine was built in 1920 to honor him and his empress: In accordance with the beliefs of the day, they had been declared divine. The shrine was destroyed by fire in the 1945 air raids, but rebuilt in the original classical design. The great *torii* (gate) is made from 1,700-year-old cypress trees from Taiwan.

Occasions Babies dressed in their best are usually brought by proud parents on Sunday and Thursday, and you can often see wedding processions–some in traditional costume and some in Western dress. The main festival is on November 3, Emperor Meiji's birthday, now known as Culture Day, when medals are awarded to those who have contributed significantly to the national culture.

Inner gardens The 150-acre (60ha) inner gardens are noted for more than 100,000 trees, sent from all over Japan when the gardens were created in 1920. The Treasure Museum at the northern end of the gardens houses royal clothes and possessions. There is also a traditional teahouse, ancient well, peaceful ponds and an iris garden.

THE BASICS

- D6
- 1-1 Yoyogi, Shibuya-ku
- 3379–5511
- Daily dawn–dusk; closed third Fri of each month
- Meijijingu-mae
- Harajuku, Sangubashi
- Few
- Free

HIGHLIGHTS

- 175 acres (70 ha) of wooded park
- Giant *torii* (gate)
- Shrine hall of cypress wood
- Folded paper prayers on bushes
- Cherry blossoms in spring
- Iris garden in summer
- Winter ice carvings
- Treasure Museum
- Wedding processions

TIP

- Take a look at the hundreds of handwritten prayer plaques–you can even write your own.

Metropolitan Government Offices

HIGHLIGHTS

- 45th-floor observatories
- Views of city and parks and glimpse of Mount Fuji (1 day in 5)
- Multiscreen video history
- Sculptures in plaza
- Granite exterior—white from Spain, dark from Sweden

TIP

- For the best view of Mount Fuji and surrounds, visit the towers on a clear day.

These striking, grandiose towers were planned in the booming 1980s, and opened in 1991. On a clear day the view from the top is unrivaled, with impressive silver and black towers rising all around.

Vantage point Each of the twin towers of Building No. 1 has an observatory on the 45th floor. It makes no difference which tower you choose: The lifts whisk you to the top in less than a minute. On a clear day the view is the most spectacular in Tokyo, with futuristic skyscrapers in the foreground, the green islands of the Meiji Shrine Inner Garden and Shinjuku Garden beyond, and the Imperial Palace, Ginza and Tokyo Bay to the east. If you are lucky, you'll see Mount Fuji's perfect cone far away on the southwestern horizon. The tourist

Shinjuku Metropolitan Government Buildings Plaza (far left); the Blacken Spouts sculpture by Churyo Sato (top middle); view from the government buildings' observation deck (top right); inside the observation deck (below left); exterior view of the government buildings (below middle); view over Yoyogi Park (below right)

information center on the first floor is open 9.30–6.30 daily.

Growth area In the days of the shogunate, Shinjuku was a day's march from the capital, Edo (now Tokyo). Weary travelers would stop at its inns to bathe and rest, dine and visit one of the many houses of pleasure. With the coming of the railroad, Shinjuku became a major junction. As late as 1970, Shinjuku was known mainly for its station, red-light district and sewage treatment works. When investors looked for alternatives to central Tokyo, Shinjuku had an important advantage: It seemed to survive earthquakes better than other areas. When the city government decided to move to Shinjuku it commissioned Kenzo Tange to design a new complex to house the offices, on a scale to match its multitrillion-yen annual budget.

THE BASICS

www.metro.tokyo.jp
C4
Tokyo Metropolitan Government Offices, 2-8-1 Nishi-Shinjuku, Shinjuku-ku
5321–3077
Daily 9.30am–10pm; closed Dec 29–Jan 3
Snack bar on 45th floor; restaurants nearby
Shinjuku
Shinjuku Tochomae
Very good
Free

Shinjuku Gyoen National Garden

HIGHLIGHTS

- Landscaped gardens
- Ponds, bridges and traditional teahouse
- Japanese, French and English gardens
- Greenhouse of tropical plants and flowers
- Chrysanthemum shows
- Picnic parties under the spring blossoms

TIP

- Bring a *bento* box and have a picnic on one of the park's immaculate lawns.

Expansive and verdant, the 150-acre (60ha) Shinjuku Gyoen National Garden is the perfect place for a stroll, especially in April when thousands come to walk and picnic under some 1,500 of their beloved flowering cherry trees.

Origins Shinjuku garden is one of the surpisingly large green spaces that relieve the concrete monotony of the city. It was once part of the estate of the powerful leader (*daimyo*) of the Naito clan, an area of land around the Edo stronghold given to the clan by the shogun Ieyasu Tokugawa to defend the approaches to the castle. Following the overthrow of the shogunate and restoration of imperial power in 1868, it came into the hands of the emperor and was completed as an imperial garden in 1906. The gardens were

Strolling in the French Garden (far left); spectacular glass house in the Shinjuku Gyoen National Garden (top right); perfect rose in the French Garden (below middle); a party of children stop on the bridge in the Japanese Garden (below right)

destroyed during World War II, but were replanted and opened to the public as a national garden in 1949.

Garden sights Landscaped with little hills, ponds and bridges, the garden includes an English landscape garden, a French formal garden and a Japanese traditional garden with a Chinese-style pavilion, where you can enjoy tea and sweet cakes. Each April, at cherry-blossom time, large crowds—guided by the daily blossom reports on TV—are drawn to admire 1,500-plus cherry trees, their white or pink petals blowing like snow in the wind. In early November, the biggest, most perfect blooms of Japan's national flower, the chrysanthemum, are on show. The popular tropical greenhouse is being rebuilt and is due to reopen in 2011.

THE BASICS

www.env.go.jp/garden/shinjukugyoen/english/index.html

E5

11 Naitocho, Shinjuku-ku

3350–0151

Tue–Sun 9–4; closed Mon except at cherry-blossom time

Snacks

Shinjuku Gyoen-mae. Take the south exit and turn right

Shinjuku

Few

Inexpensive

More to See

HANAZONO SHRINE

Now surrounded by the monuments of commerce and pleasure, this is one of the oldest shrines in Tokyo. People pray here for success in business.

D4 Opposite Marui Interior store, Shinjuku Sanchome, Shinjuku-ku Daily dawn–9pm Plenty nearby Shinjuku Sanchome Free

JAPANESE SWORD MUSEUM

Gleaming and flawless, the blades kept in this museum are up to 900 years old. They are deadly weapons transmuted by age and beauty into works of art. You really can see why they were credited with magical power.

C5 4-25-10 Yoyogi, Shibuya-ku 3379–1386 Tue–Sun 9–4; closed Dec 28–Jan 4 Nearby Sangubashi Moderate

KEIO PLAZA HOTEL 45TH FLOOR

The rooftop of the first skyscraper to be built in Shinjuku is a spectacular vantage point. At night, the window seats in the hotel's penthouse cocktail bars wouldn't suit sufferers from vertigo, and the prices are similarly elevated.

C4 2-2-1 Nishi-Shinjuku, Shinjuku-ku 3344–0111 Daily 5–11pm Snacks, plus many restaurants in hotel Shinjuku Moderate

NHK BROADCASTING CENTER

NHK runs tours of the sets used for their TV programs. Performances are in Japanese.

C7 2-2-1 Jinnan, Shibuya-ku 5400–6900 Tue–Sun 10–6; closed Tue if Mon is a national holiday Snacks Meijijingu-mae Shibuya Moderate

NIHON MINGEIKAN (JAPAN FOLK CRAFTS MUSEUM)

This museum was founded by one of Japan's leading philosophers and critics, Soetsu Yanagi. He campaigned to preserve *mingei*, the term he coined to describe the "art of the people." The museum is dedicated to the intrinsic beauty of crafts made for

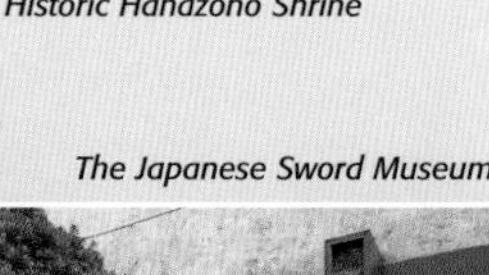

Historic Hanazono Shrine

The Japanese Sword Museum

daily use. Exhibitions are rotated four times a year to allow all the examples of pottery, textiles, carvings, furniture and kitchen equipment to be shown.
B7 4-3-33 Komaba, Meguro-ku 3467–4527 Tue–Sun 10–5; closed Dec 22–Jan 3 Komabatodai-mae Moderate

NTT INTERCOMMUNICATION CENTER

Science and art converge in this exhibition and interactive display of computer graphics. The "cave" filled with modifiable 3-D imagery is most spectacular. Communication media is what it's all about.
C5 Tokyo Opera City Tower 4F, 3-20-2 Nishi-Shinjuku, Shinjuku-ku 0120–144199 (toll-free) Tue–Sun 10–6 Café Shinjuku Moderate

OTA MEMORIAL MUSEUM OF ART

At this museum you have to exchange your shoes for slippers. The *ukiyo-e* prints, and the original paintings from which they were made, were collected by business magnate Seizo Ota (1893–1977). He amassed 10,000 examples, and the museum has since acquired more, so displays are rotated.
D6 1-10-10 Jingumae, Shibuya-ku 5777–8600 Tue–Sun 10.30–5.30; closed from 26th to end of each month and Dec 19–Jan 2 Drinks and snacks in basement Meijijingu-mae Harajuku Moderate

SEIJI TOGO MEMORIAL ART MUSEUM

Many of the paintings on show here are by Seiji Togo (1897–1978), whose work depicts the grace and beauty of Japanese women. The museum made headlines when it paid a world-record price for Van Gogh's *Sunflowers* in 1987, and is noted for its 33 pictures by the American primitive artist, Grandma Moses.
C4 1-26-1 Nishi-Shinjuku, Shinjuku-ku 3349–3080 Tue–Sun 9.30–5; closed Dec 27–Jan 4 Restaurants in same building Shinjuku Shinjuku Moderate

A pleasant corner at the Japan Folk Crafts Museum

The imposing Seiji Togo Memorial Museum of Art

SHINJUKU STATION

Twice a day, a tidal wave of humanity pours through Japan's busiest station—3 to 4 million commuters, shoppers and schoolchildren stream along its passages, heading for a dozen exits and changing trains. Subway lines and JR railroad lines meet at Shinjuku; private lines feed customers to their own department stores right above the station. The famous people-pushers operate at rush hour (*rashawa* in Japanese), packing as many bodies as they can into each carriage, giving them a final shove to let the doors close and then bowing as the train pulls out. It's worth experiencing—once—but not as an introduction to the system. Learn your way around at a quieter time first.

You can walk more than half a mile (1km) underground (more if you get lost). Here and there, the homeless, who have somehow dropped through the cracks of Japan's tightly knit society, find a place to sleep, cocooned in cardboard cartons. The east exit leads to the My City building with several stories of good eating places and into a maze of alleys and the night entertainment of Kabukicho.

D4 · Shinjuku-ku · 4.30am–11.30pm · Innumerable eating places of every kind · Shinjuku · Shinjuku · Free

SUMITOMO TOWER

This 52-story, six-sided building with a hollow center has a lookout point, and the top three floors are given over to restaurants used by office workers for lunch, some staying open in the evening. Window tables have the kind of view you might get from a spaceship.

C4 · 2-6-1 Nishi-Shinjuku, Shinjuku-ku · Daily 9am–10pm · Many restaurants · Shinjuku · Free

TEPCO ELECTRIC ENERGY MUSEUM

This museum run by the Tokyo Electric Power Company has seven floors of interactive exhibits.

D7 · 1-12-10 Jinnan, Shibuya-ku · 3477-1191 · Thu–Tue 10–6 · Shibuya · Free

People-pushers at work during rush hour at Shinjuku station

Interior view of the Sumitomo Tower

TOGO SHRINE

Set amid gardens and overlooking a lake, the shrine is a tribute to Admiral Togo, Japan's naval hero in the 1905 destruction of the Russian fleet at Tsushima. Tokyo's largest antiques market is held here on the 1st, 4th and 5th Sunday of the month.

D6 · Off Meiji-dori, Harajuku, Shibuya-ku · 3403–3591 · Daily dawn–dusk · Meijijingu-mae · Free

TOKYO OPERA CITY

An arts complex comprising a 54-story tower with theaters, event halls, an art gallery for special exhibitions, business and commercial facilities and shops, bars and restaurants. The adjoining New National Theater hosts opera, ballet, drama and dance.

C5 · 3-20-2, Nishi-Shinjuku, Shinjuku-ku · 5353–0700 · Daily 9–9 · Shinjuku · Moderate

WATARI MUSEUM OF CONTEMPORARY ART

This small gallery specializes in cutting-edge art with new exhibitions put on every few months. It hosts regular lectures and runs workshops for artists. Specialist exhibitions include photography and architecture. The gift shop sells sketchbooks, photo albums, a huge selection of art postcards and arty T-shirts.

E6 · 3-7-6 Jingumae, Shibuya-ku · 3402–3001 · Tue 11–7, Wed 11–9, Thu–Sun 11–7 · Café · Gaienmae · Moderate

YOYOGI PARK

Once an imperial army training ground, then renamed Washington Heights by the US occupation forces who used it for housing, the area became the site of the 1964 Olympic village and was renamed Yoyogi Park. The park's paths, lawns and wooded areas are pleasant to stroll through. The National Yoyogi Sports Center and Stadium, just across the road, was also created for the Games. Its stadium's pillarless roof is still strikingly modern.

C6 · Yoyogi, Shibuya-ku · Daily 5–5 · Snacks · Meijijingu-mae, Harajuku · Free

People enjoying the fresh air and fountains in Yoyogi Park

Classical musicians perform at a Shinto ceremony at Togo Shrine

Harajuku to Omotesando

This walk takes in Tokyo's grandest Shinto shrine, funky Takeshita-dori and the impressive Omotesando-dori.

DISTANCE: 3 miles (5km) **ALLOW:** 4 hours

START

HARAJUKU STATION

D6 Harajuku station

❶ From the station follow the signs to the Meiji Jingu Shrine (▷ 25), a pretty 654-yard (600m) walk through the forest, under a giant *torii* (gate) made from ancient cypress trees.

❷ Arriving at the shrine, rebuilt in classic style after it was destroyed by US warplanes in World War II, observe the wooden votive plaques near the entrance.

❸ You may choose to take a 545-yard (500m) walk north to the Treasure Museum, which houses royal clothes and possessions.

❹ Head back to Harajuku station and take the exit to Takeshita-dori (▷ 24). Amble this narrow street and its side lanes and marvel at the merchandise on sale.

❺ Next, head toward the wide, tree-lined Omotesando-dori.

❻ On the way, divert to Jingumae where the small Ota Memorial Museum of Art (▷ 31) houses important examples of early Japanese woodblock prints by such masters as Hiroshige and Hokusai.

❼ Back in Omotesando-dori, before you take the 1.2-mile (2km) stroll to the station, you might pause at one of the many Parisian-style cafés for a sit-down break and a coffee and a chance to watch the locals pass by.

❽ Stop off at Daiso Harajuku (▷ 35), one of the largest ¥100 shops in Tokyo, for a bargain. Omotesando station is 212 yards (200m) farther.

OMOTESANDO STATION

E7 Omotesando station

END

Shopping

AOYAMA OVAL PLAZA
Over 45 dealers offer a fascinating variety of antiques, ranging from expensive treasures to souvenir items.
E7 Near National Children's Castle, 5-52-2 Jingumae, Shibuya-ku Every 3rd Sat of month 6–sunset Omotesando

BINGO YA
Folk art, crafts, traditional toys and gifts from all parts of Japan.
D4 10-6 Wakamatsu-cho, Shinjuku-ku 3202–8778 Thu–Sun 10–7 Shinjuku

DAISO HARAJUKU
This ¥100 shop is one of the largest in Tokyo. A great place to buy inexpensive tableware.
D6 1-19-24 Jingumae, Shibuya-ku 5775–9641 Daily 10–9 Harajuku

LAFORÊT
A trendy shopping complex with seven floors of shops and fashion boutiques.
D6 1-11-16 Jingumae, Shibuya-ku 5414–3628 Daily 11–8 Meijijingu-mae

FUJI-TORII
Established in 1948, this reputable dealer carries quality antiques and works of art.
D6 6-1-10 Jingumae, Shibuya-ku 3400–2777 Wed–Mon 11–6 Meijijingu-mae

HMV
This store has tens of thousands of CDs, cassettes and DVDs in stock.
D7 24-1 Udagawacho, Shibuya 5458–3411 Daily 10–10 Shibuya

ISETAN
An enormous store above Shinjuku-sanchome station, with dozens of designer boutiques. The food hall and restaurants are in the basement.
D4 3-14-1 Shinjuku, Shinjuku-ku 3352–1111 Daily 10–10 Shinjuku

KIDDYLAND
Sells the toys, alarm clocks and kitsch that childhood dreams are made of.
D6 6-1-9 Jingumae, Shibuya-ku 3409–3431 Daily 10–9 Harajuku Meijijingu-mae

PRICE OF PARADISE

The shops are a pleasure to visit, the range and quality of goods outstanding, the displays beautiful, the service usually impeccable. The customer is always right. Your most mundane purchase will be wrapped as though it were a jewel beyond price. Inflation has been low for decades and, with most foreign currencies increasing in value compared with the yen in recent years, prices are much more reasonable than they used to be.

KINOKUNIYA
A large stock of foreign books is on the 6th floor.
D4 Annex Building, Times Square, 5-24-2 Sendagaya, Shibuya-ku 5361–3301 Daily 10–8 Shinjuku

ORIENTAL BAZAAR
Four levels of handicrafts, souvenirs, antiques, bric-a-brac, dolls and kimonos.
E7 5-9-13 Jingumae, Shibuya-ku 3400–3933 Fri–Wed 9.30–6.30 Omotesando

SEIBU
Designer boutiques, children's wear, stationery.
D7 21-1 Udagawa-cho, Shibuya-ku 3462–0111 Thu–Tue 10–8.30 Shibuya

TOGO SHRINE
Bargain for antiques along the sidewalk in the shrine's gardens.
D6 Harajuku, Shibuya-ku Every 1st, 4th and 5th Sun of month 4am–5pm Meijijingu-mae

TOKYU
The latest fashions for younger customers and a great basement food hall.
D7 2-24 Dogenzaka, Shibuya-ku 3477–3111 Daily 10–8 Shibuya

TOKYU HANDS
Everything you need for model-making, sewing, carpentry and more.
D7 12-18 Udagawacho, Shibuya-ku 5489–5111 Daily 10–7 Shibuya

Entertainment and Nightlife

BEER STATION
One of Tokyo's most popular beer halls. A choice of tables or beer counters from where you order a variety of beers and snacks.
D9 Yebisu Garden Place, 4-20-1 Ebisu, Shibuya-ku 3422–9731 Mon–Sat 11.30–11, Sun, hols 11.30–10 Ebisu

BELGO
Over 130 brands of European beers on tap and a wide variety of Belgian dishes, including wine-steamed mussels and venison carpaccio.
D7 3-18-7 Shibuya-ku, Shibuya 3409–4442 Daily 5.30–2am; closed some Sun Shibuya Moderate

BUNKAMURA ORCHARD HALL
Part of an impressive cultural center, with a cinema and theaters featuring musicals, concerts and events.
D7 2-24-1 Dogenzaka, Shibuya-ku 3477–9111 Shibuya

CERULEAN TOWER NOH THEATER
Japanese traditional performing arts, including noh (▷ panel, 48), are shown in a small noh theater, and there are restaurants and shops.
D7 31-2, Sakuragaoka-cho, Shibuya-ku 3476–3000 Mon–Sun 8am–11pm Shibuya Moderate

CINE AMUSE EAST AND WEST
Cinema showing the latest Western and Asian releases.
D7 Fontis Building, 4F, 2-23-12 Dogenzaka, Shibuya-ku 3496–2888 Mon–Sun 10am–11pm Shibuya Moderate

KANZE NOH-GAKUDO
Regular noh performances are held here.
D7 1-16-4 Shoto, Shibuya-ku 3469–5241 Shibuya

LA FABRIQUE
One of Tokyo's smaller clubs, La Fabrique has one of the best sound systems and music varies depending on the night, although Progressive House and Garage are popular.
D7 1-16-9 Udagawa-cho, Shibuya-ku 5428–5100 Daily 9pm–3am Shibuya Expensive

KABUKI
Kabuki developed under the Tokugawa shoguns, and two prohibitions gave it the character is still has today. In 1629, women were banned from the stage, resulting in the tradition of *onnagata*–male actors specializing in female roles. Then it was forbidden to attend the plays wearing swords. The samurai class, who wouldn't be seen in public without a sword, stayed away, and kabuki became an entertainment for the masses. The plays blend historical romance, tragedy and comedy, music, dance and acrobatics, performed in vivid costumes and make-up.

NEW NATIONAL THEATER TOKYO (NNTT)
This state-of-the-art venue has three theaters: the Opera House, the Pit, and the Play House, where you can enjoy contemporary dance, drama, opera and ballet. There are also backstage tours.
B5 1-1-1 Honmachi, Shibuya-ku 5351–3011 Hatsudai Moderate to expensive

TOKYO OPERA CITY
Despite its name, this new theater and art gallery complex presents a varied orchestral concert program.
B5 B3-20-2 Nishi-Shinjuku, Shinjuku-ku 5353–0770 Hatsudai Moderate to expensive

WOMB
Trendy nightspot for Techno and Progressive House fans. The Obi Lounge is a great place for a quiet drink and bite to eat. ID card with picture required on entry.
D7 2-16 Maruyamacho, Shibuya-ku 5459–0039 Daily 9pm–3am Shibuya Expensive

Restaurants

PRICES

Prices are approximate, based on a 3-course meal for one person.

¥¥¥	over ¥8,000
¥¥	¥3,000–¥8,000
¥	under ¥3,000

ASAHI ZUSHI (¥¥)
A friendly, reliable Japanese restaurant in the Tokyu department store. Reasonable prices, contemporary setting.
D7 2-24-1 Tokyu Department Store, 9F, Shibuya-ku 3477–4821 Daily 10–8; closed Thu Shibuya

BISTRO DE MAIDO (¥¥)
Western dishes with a local twist. An informal restaurant that's popular with young business-people. Salads topped with lightly salted seafoods are a specialty.
D7 Miyagi Building B1, 1-10-12 Shibuya, Shibuya-ku 3407–5724 Daily 5.30pm–11.30pm; closed 31 Dec–4 Jan Shibuya

IL BOCCALONE (¥¥¥)
A north Italian-style trattoria, with good antipasti and grills and notable desserts.
D9 1-15-9 Ebisu, Shibuya-ku 3449–1430 Mon–Sat 5.30–11 Ebisu

LA BOHÈME (¥)
Various pastas and sauces, pizzas, salads and ice creams. Popular with night owls.
E7 Jubilee Plaza B1F, 5-8-5 Jingumae, Shibuya-ku 5467–5666 Daily 11.30am–5am Omotesando

BOUGAINVILLEA (¥¥)
This place has a wide choice of authentic Vietnamese dishes, including noodle soups, crab with coriander, spring rolls, sweet-and-sour pork or chicken and meatballs.
D7 Romanee Building 2F, 2-25-9 Dogenzaka, Shibuya-ku 3496–5537 Daily 5–11 Shibuya

CARMINE EDOCHIANO (¥)
Italy meets Japan–Tuscan cuisine in a genteel old Japanese house. The setting alone makes it worth a visit.
F4 9-13 Arakicho, Shinjuku-ku 3225–6767 Daily 11.30–2, 6–9.30 Yotsuya-sanchome

EL CASTELLANO (¥¥)
An informal and high-spirited Spanish establishment with a variety of tapas, tortillas and wonderful paella. This is one of the few restaurants in Japan to serve rabbit.
D7 2-9-12 Shibuya, Omotesando 3407–7197 Mon–Sat 6pm–10pm Shibuya

CHANG-PLAI (¥¥)
Bangkok-style café that features a large menu of tasty street-stand style fare. The adventurous chef is creative with his special dishes. The atmosphere is casual and friendly and prices are very reasonable.
D9 1-14-15 Ebisu-Minami, Shibuya-ku 3715–4588 Daily 5pm–10.30pm Ebisu

LAS CHICAS (¥¥)
This café/bar has an English-language menu featuring international cuisine including vegetarian dishes, salads and pizzas.
E7 5-47-6 Jingumae, Shibuya-ku 3407–6865 Daily 11–11 Omotesando

DOLE FRUIT CAFÉ (¥)
Fresh fruits and vegetables come as juices, and in tasty combinations in curries and pizzas. Many vegetarian dishes.
D7 Kokusai Building A-Kan 2F, 13-16 Udagawacho, Shibuya-ku 3464–6030 Daily 11–10 Shibuya

GOOD HONEST GRUB (¥)
A friendly place for brunch. Fresh fruit and vegetable juices plus vegetarian dishes.
D9 1-11-11 Ebisu-Minami, Shibuya-ku 3710–0400 Mon–Fri 11.30–11, Sat–Sun, national holidays 9–4.30pm, dinner until 11pm Ebisu

HACHIUTA (¥¥)
Delicious tofu, stir-fry and selected neo-Japanese

dishes are all prepared with the freshest of ingredients. You will find a selection of French and Italian wines available here. English is spoken by the staff.
D7 38-3 Udagawacho, Shibuya-ku 3496–8009 Daily 5am–11pm Shibuya

KAKIYA SUSHI (¥)
This stylish restaurant serves excellent, high-quality sushi.
D6 1-14-27 Jingumae, Shibuya-ku 3423–1400 Daily 11–10.30 Harajuku

MAIMON (¥¥)
Try the regional sake, along with oysters and delicious grilled chicken.
D7 15-1 Udagawacho, Parco P. I, 8F, Shibuya-ku 3464–6644 Daily 11am–midnight Shibuya

MAISEN (¥)
Located in a converted bathhouse, diners come for the house special *tonkatsu* (deep-fried pork cutlets). Miso soup, rice and cabbage are included in the set dishes.
E7 4-8-5 Jingumae, Shibuya-ku 3470–0071 Mon–Sat lunch, dinner Omotesando

MAI-THAI (¥¥)
This is a small, cheerful, popular spot in a side street, serving a typical Thai menu at reasonable prices.
D9 1-18-16 Ebisu, Shibuya-ku 3280–1155 Daily 5.30pm–10pm Ebisu

MYOKO (¥)
The house specialty is *hoto* (wide, flat udon noodles). Try the hot *hoto nabe* with miso broth and vegetables.
D7 Shinto Building 1F, 1-17-2 Shibuya, Shibuya-ku 3499–3450 Daily 11–9.30 Shibuya

NEGISHI (¥)
Tasty country-style beef dishes are served at this rustic budget eatery.
D4 2-45-2 Kabukicho, Shinjuku-ku 3232–8020 Daily 11–3, 5–12 Shinjuku

CHOICES

Bento: Box lunch.
Miso: Soybean paste.
Ramen: Chinese noodles, in soups, usually with pork.
Shabu-shabu: Thin slices of beef swirled in a boiling broth, then dipped in sauces.
Soba: Buckwheat noodles.
Sukiyaki: Thinly sliced beef cooked at the table with vegetables and tofu.
Teishoku: Fixed-price menu.
Tempura: Shrimps, fish and vegetables coated in light batter and deep fried.
Teppanyaki: Fish, meat, vegetables cooked on a griddle.
Udon: Wheat-flour noodles.
Yakitori: Small pieces of chicken, liver or other meat, grilled on bamboo skewers.

PALETTE (¥)
A plain café where Sri Lankan chefs make the curries as hot as you choose. Breads and desserts are excellent.
D9 1-15-2 Ebisu-Nishi, Shibuya-ku 5489–0770 Mon–Sat 11.30–3, 5.30–11.30 Ebisu

ROSITA (¥)
Guacamole, tacos, enchiladas, chilli con carne and other Mexican basics. The ambience is very folksy.
D4 Pegasus-Kan Building B1, 3-31-5 Shinjuku, Shinjuku-ku 3356–7538 Daily 12–11 Shinjuku-sanchome

SAMOVAR (¥¥)
Authentic Russian stews and soups, kebabs and rye bread. Plenty of beers and vodkas.
D7 2-22-5 Dogenzaka, Shibuya-ku 3462–0648 Mon–Sat 5pm–11pm Shibuya

TANDOOR (¥)
Good range of spicy meat and vegetarian curries. The surroundings may be basic but the service is friendly.
D9 1-9-3 Ebisu-Nishi, Shibuya-ku 3461–6181 Daily 11–10 Ebisu

TSUNAHACHI (¥)
Fine tempura at a surprisingly fair price, but stick to the set menus.
D4 3-31-8 Shinjuku, Shinjuku-ku 3352–1012 Daily 11.15–10 Shinjuku-Sanchome

Around Roppongi

Popular Roppongi is at the heart of the Minato-ku district. To get your bearings, take the elevator to the observation deck of the Roppongi Hills tower, then shop, dine and spend the evening in the district.

Sights	**42–46**
Shopping	**47**
Entertainment and Nightlife	**48**
Restaurants	**49–50**

Top 25 TOP 25

Roppongi Hills ▷ **42**
Sengakuji Temple ▷ **44**
Yebisu Garden Place ▷ **45**

5
6
7
8
9
D
E
F
Aoyama Cemetery
Nogizaka
MINAMI-AOYAMA
GAIEN-NISHI-DŌRI
OMOTESANDO AVE
SEIJO
Taro Okamoto Memorial Museum
Nezu Institute of Fine Arts
KOTTŌ-DŌRI
ROPPONGI-DŌRI
3
EXPRESSWAY
Aoyamagakuin University
NISHI-AZABU
Jissen Joshi-gakuen
KOMAZAWA-DŌRI
HACHIMAN-DŌRI
HIGASHI
HIROO
GAIEN-NISHI-DŌRI
Tōkyō Metropolitan Central Library
Hiroo
Arisugawa Memorial Park
EBISU-NISHI
MEIJI-DŌRI
DAIKAN-YAMA
Shibuya
Ebisu
KOMAZAWA-DŌRI
EBISU STATION
EBISU
2
Beer Museum
Westin Tokyo Hotel
EBISU-MINAMI
EXPRESSWAY
NAKA-MEGURO
Yebisu Garden Place
Tokyo Metropolitan Museum of Photography
0
250 m
0
250 yds
MITA
National Park for Nature Study

Around Roppongi

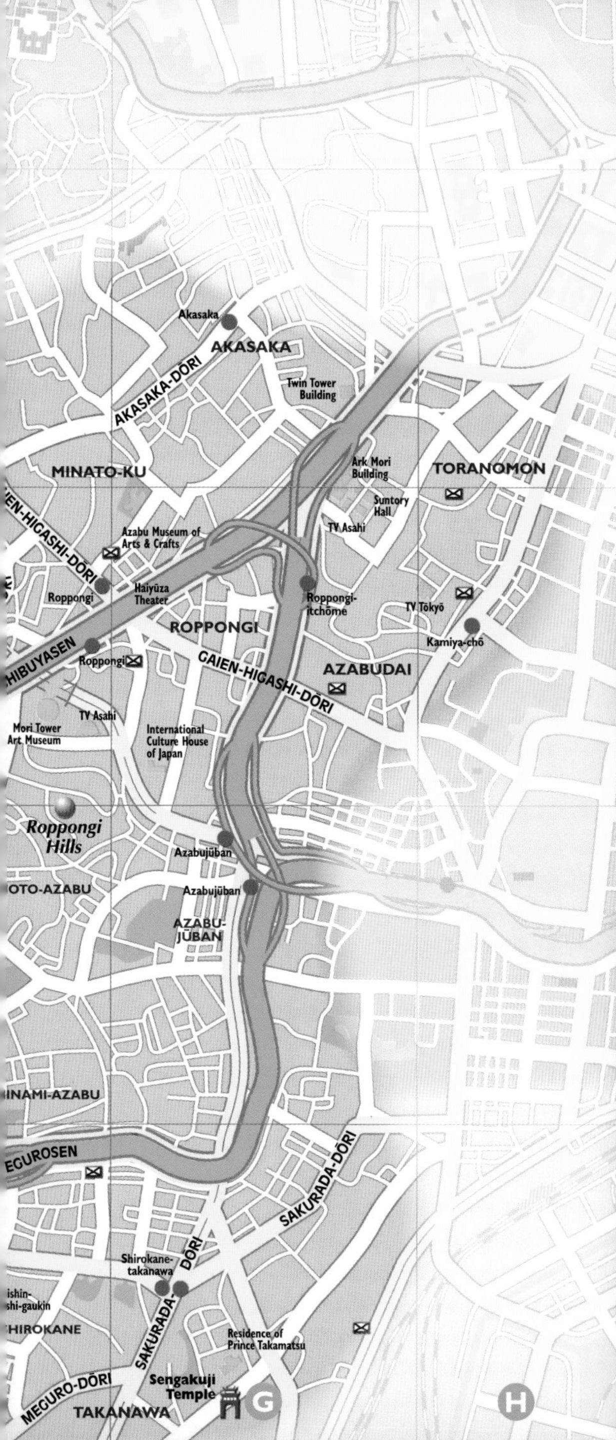

Roppongi Hills

Café scene at Roppongi (left); at the top of the Mori Tower (below); Roppongi Mori Tower (right)

THE BASICS

www.roppongihills.com/en
F8
Mori Tower, 6-10-1 Roppongi, Minato-ku
6406–6000; Tokyo City View 6406–6652
Daily 9am–1am
Roppongi
Good
Free; Tokyo City View expensive

HIGHLIGHTS

- Cutting-edge design
- Tokyo City View
- Mori Art Center
- Public art
- Landscaped open areas
- Brand-name shops
- Variety of dining

This stunning new precinct, with its central 54-story (780ft/238m) main tower building, includes an urban art gallery, dramatic observation deck, brand-name shops, public art, tranquil open spaces and busy plazas.

Grand scale Covering approximately 11 acres (4ha), with a total floor area of 7,790,240sq ft (724,000sq m), Roppongi Hills is Japan's largest urban redevelopment project. By cleverly integrating office, residential, hotel, retail and cultural facilities with parks and plazas, the architect has drawn locals, expatriates and visitors in droves to this complex that surprises and delights at every turn. A shopping and dining plaza links directly to Roppongi subway station, while a mixed-use building offers commercial and educational facilities, the 390-room five-star Grand Hyatt Tokyo, TV Asahi's broadcasting center and a theater for the performing arts. Shopping options include all the top designer names. Be sure to have a drink in the Bamboo Bar on level 5.

More to see Tokyo City View 1,148ft (350m) above sea level offers great views of the city on a clear day or of sparkling lights at night. Mori Art Center, the world's first institution affiliated with the Museum of Modern Art in New York, is on the same level and admission charges include access to this cutting-edge gallery that specializes in art, urban design and city architecture. The museum shops and the Roppongi Hills Art and Design store sell art and design products and books.

Sengakuji Temple

Worshippers at the *ronin* tombs (left); statue at the entrance (middle); the Oishi tomb (right)

THE BASICS

G9
2-11-1 Takanawa, Minato-ku
3441–5560
Daily 9–5
Small restaurants in nearby street
Sengakuji (exit A2 and head uphill)
Few
Temple free. Museum inexpensive

HIGHLIGHTS

- Sanmon, the main gate
- Shoro, the Bell Tower
- Tombs of the 47 *ronin*
- Tombs of Asano and Oishi
- Temple gardens
- Polychrome statues of the 47 *ronin*
- Samurai weapons and armor
- Original clothing

This temple offers an insight into Japanese values: The heroes are honored for their loyalty, efficiency, ruthlessness and collective action. They lived and died by the samurai code.

Code of honor Sengakuji was one of the three great temples of Edo, and it is still one of the most important in Tokyo. After their lord Asano Takuminokami was unjustly forced into suicide in 1701, Yoshitaka Oishi and 47 loyal retainers (*ronin*, meaning "masterless samurai") vowed to avenge him. They raided the castle of the chief instigator, Yoshinaka Kira, beheaded him, and carried the head in triumph to Asano's tomb at Sengakuji. They in turn were required by their code to commit ritual suicide, a duty they accepted as an honor. Before killing himself, Oishi chivalrously returned Kira's head to his family. The receipt for "one head" signed by the temple priests can be seen in the museum. The story has been told as kabuki (▷ 36) and puppet theater, in movies and on television.

The tombs and museum Oishi and his followers were buried at Sengakuji. The 47 simple stones are arranged in a square, with the larger tombs of Asano and his wife, and Oishi and his son, nearby. Clouds of smoke rise from incense sticks placed in front of each tomb by the many worshippers who come to honor the dead heroes. In the museum, there are polychrome statues believed to be exact likenesses of Oishi and his son. Their armor and weapons are displayed separately.

Exterior of the Beer Station (left); Central Square at Yebisu Garden Place (right)

Yebisu Garden Place

The old Sapporo Brewery site is one of the city's most imaginative developments—a luxury hotel, two brilliantly designed museums, a shopping complex and, from atop Yebisu Garden Place Tower, sweeping city views.

The beer connection As a serious polluter, the redbrick brewery had to go, but the company held onto the site, moved its offices here, and created 1,000 luxury apartments. Some of the brewing equipment went into a beer museum (▷ 46), where it takes on the quality of sculpture. The brewing process is explained and in a virtual reality brewery tour you see what it's like to be a molecule going through fermentation. Then you get to sample a glass of the product.

Time out Check out the Tokyo Metropolitan Museum of Photography (▷ 46) while you're here too. And browse the Mitsukoshi department store, or try the restaurant complex with a huge beer hall reminiscent of a Munich *Bierkeller* of the 1930s. Window-shoppers might want to check out the Glass Square complex. The Westin Tokyo Hotel is worth a visit; there's a good view from the bar or restaurant on the 22nd floor. For an even better vantage point, head for the 38th and 39th floors of the Yebisu Garden Place Tower. You can enjoy lunch, dinner or even just snacks at the many restaurants at these two levels, but if you've already been tempted by the large collection of Japanese, Western and tavern-type eateries on the ground level, you can visit for the views alone.

THE BASICS

www.gardenplace.co.jp/english
E9
4-20-3 Ebisu, Shibuya-ku
General information: 5423–7111
Mon–Wed, Sat–Sun 11–7, Thu–Fri 11–8; museums closed Mon. Restaurant hours vary
Beer hall, restaurants, fast-food outlets
Ebisu Ebisu
Good
Free (except Museum of Photography; ▷ 46)
Chain of moving walkways from JR Ebisu station

HIGHLIGHTS

- Beer Museum
- Museum of Photography (▷ 46)
- Mitsukoshi department store
- "Top of Yebisu" views
- Westin Tokyo Hotel (▷ 46)
- 1930s-style German beer hall

More to See

BEER MUSEUM

This feature of Yebisu Garden Place (▷ 45) can be reached by moving walkways from Ebisu JR station. The Sapporo brewery is now closed, but you can see the brewing process via virtual reality headsets. The museum's collection of advertising posters includes a gauze-clad beauty of 1908.

E9 4-20-1 Ebisu, Shibuya-ku 5423–7255 Tue–Sun 10–6; closed Mon and Dec 28–Jan 4 Huge beer hall, restaurants and fast-food outlets Ebisu Free

NEZU INSTITUTE OF FINE ARTS

www.nezu-muse.or.jp/index_e.html

The institute houses Japanese, Chinese and Korean fine arts collected by businessman Kaichiro Nezu. The gallery is in its own beautiful gardens Currently closed for renovation, it is due to reopen late in 2009.

E7 6-5-1 Minami-Aoyama, Minato-ku 3400–2536 Tue–Sun 9.30–4.30; closed day after national holidays Café Gazebo Omotesando (10-min walk) Expensive

TOKYO METROPOLITAN MUSEUM OF PHOTOGRAPHY

The museum is part of the Yebisu Garden Place development (▷ 45). Early photographs on show include some from before the Meiji Restoration of 1868. Imaginative displays demonstrate time-honored optical illusions and their modern equivalent, holography. The Images and Technology Gallery includes displays of animation and cinematography.

E9 1-13-3 Mita, Meguro-ku 3280–0099 Tue–Wed, Sun 10–6, Sat, Thu–Fri 10–8; closed Tue if Mon is a national holiday and Dec 28–Jan 4 Coffee shop Ebisu Moderate

WESTIN TOKYO HOTEL

From the 22nd-floor bar and restaurant here, and at the top of Yebisu in the same complex, look out on Yebisu Garden Place (▷ 45), north to Shibuya, and east to Shinagawa.

E9 Yebisu Garden Place, 1-4-1 Mita, Meguro-ku 5423–7000 Daily 11am–midnight Bar and restaurant Ebisu

A gleaming mash copper in the Beer Museum

Entrance to the Tokyo Metropolitan Museum of Photography

Shopping

ANTIQUES HASEBE-YA
An eclectic stock of *tansu*, netsuke, lacquerware, and woodware—boxes, carvings and furniture.
F7 17-7 Azabu-Juban, Minato-ku 5775–1308 Daily 10–7 Roppongi

AOYAMA BOOK CENTER
Check this one out for the large stock of American and European titles and a selection of Japanese manga (comics and print cartoons).
F7 6-1-20 Roppongi, Minato-ku 3479–0479 Daily 10–10 Roppongi

AXIS
This building has more than 20 galleries featuring beautifully crafted furniture, ceramics, fabrics—everything for the discriminating interior decorator.
F7 5-17-1 Roppongi, Minato-ku 3587–2781 Mon–Sat 11–7 Roppongi

DON QUIJOTE
Tokyo's best discount store has six levels of clothing, electrical goods, CDs and DVDs, souvenirs and food. It is worth visiting just to view the variety of Japanese goods on offer. Tax free on purchases over ¥10,000.
F7 3-14-10 Roppongi, Minato-ku 5786–0811 Daily 24 hours Roppongi

KISSO
Fine ceramics combine traditional methods with modern designs. The shop shares premises with a restaurant specializing in *kaiseki* set meals.
F7 Axis Building B1F, 5-17-1, Roppongi, Minato-ku 3582–4191 Daily 11.30–2, 5.30–9 Roppongi

KUROFUNE ANTIQUES
A colorful shop, well-stocked with fine porcelain, old prints, lacquerware, furniture and folk art.
F7 7-7-4 Roppongi B1F, Minato-ku 3479–1552 Mon–Sat 10–6 Roppongi

IN-STORE FOOD

Department stores are a boon to visitors, and not only when they want to shop or to use the toilet facilities. Most stores have a whole selection of reasonably priced restaurants offering different food styles, normally on the top floor. But in the basement their food-to-go departments are an eye-opener, and an education in the ingredients of Japanese cuisine. The artistically prepared box lunches (*bento*) are a comparative bargain, and—if your budget is really restricted—you can taste all sorts of free samples, although they are more likely to sharpen your appetite than satisfy it.

MINAMI-AOYAMA
Antiques shops along and around Kotto-dori; fashion stores on Aoyama-dori and Omotesando-dori.
E7 Omotesando

NOGI SHRINE FLEA MARKET
A popular flea market specializing in antique Japanese pottery, held even in the rain.
F7 8-11-27 Akasaka, Minato-ku Every 2nd Sun of month 7–6 Nogizaka

ROPPONGI ANTIQUE BAZAAR
More than 25 dealers offer Japanese antiques to suit all budgets. Just 5 minutes' walk from Roppongi subway.
F7 5-5-1 Roppongi, Minato-ku Every 4th Thu and Fri of month 8–6 Roppongi

TASAKI PEARL GALLERY
This shop has several showrooms, and offers tours and demonstrations. City tour buses often include this on their itinerary.
G6 1-3-3 Akasaka, Minato-ku 5561–8880 Daily 9–6 Akasaka

WASHIKOBO
Washi and *mingei* (folkcraft) items.
F7 1-8-10 Nishi-Azabu, Minato-ku 3405–1841 Mon–Sat 10–6 Roppongi

Entertainment and Nightlife

AZABU JUBAN ONSEN

A nice *onsen* (thermal bath), in an unlikely location, on the first and third floors of a modern building. A natural hot spring, 1,625ft (500m) underground, is the source. Men's and women's facilities are separate.
F7 1-5-22 Azabu-Juban, Minato-ku 3404–2610 Wed–Mon 11–9 Roppongi

BLUE NOTE TOKYO

www.bluenote.co.jp/en/index.html
Internationally renowned musicians perform as you enjoy the delicious food and specialty cocktails. Very popular, book early.
E7 6-13-6 Minami-Aoyama, Minato-ku 5485–0088 Omotesando

CLUB B-FLAT TOKYO

A great jazz venue, where you can enjoy bands of all kinds and nationalities.
G6 Akasaka Sakae Building, 6-6-4 Akasaka, Minatu-ku 5563–2563 Daily 8.30–11 Akasaka

GERONIMO SHOT BAR

Legendary partying, in a Native American setting. Located right at Roppongi Crossing, next to the bookstore, two floors up.
F7 Yamamuro Bldg 2F, 7-14-10 Roppongi, Minato-ku 3478–7449 Mon–Fri 6pm–6am, Sat–Sun 7pm–6am Roppongi

MOGAMBO

www.mogambo.net
A favorite with expats and Roppongi nightlife staff. Check the website for free drink coupons and specials.
F7 Osawa Building, 1F, 6-1-7 Roppongi, Minato-ku 3403–4833 Mon–Fri 6pm–6am, Sat 7pm–6am, Sun closed Roppongi

ROPPONGI

The area is a favorite with Tokyo's foreign contingent as well as more adventurous Japanese, partly because it's still awake at 4am, when everywhere else is quiet. The Almond coffeehouse at Roppongi Crossing, near the subway station, is a popular rendezvous. There's a huge choice of eating and drinking places nearby, and the Roppongi Hills complex (▷ 42) has lots of entertainment on offer.

NOH

Much older than kabuki, infinitely stylized, and performed by masked actors, noh is less accessible still to foreigners. Even the Japanese confess to wishing it didn't go on so long, and so slowly. The younger generation says "*Noh*? No!" Listings magazines (▷ 115, 120) will tell you about the open-air, torch-lit performances at temples, where even the uninitiated can enjoy the gorgeous costumes and setting.

SALSA SUDADA

Dance lessons are on offer every day of the week–plus a free Merengue class on Fridays (7–8pm). There's no cover charge on weeknights, drink prices are reasonable and the Latin rhythms irresistible!
F7 La Pallette Building, 3F, 7-13-8 Roppongi 5474–8806 Daily 6pm–6am Roppongi

SUNTORY HALL

A fine concert hall in the Ark Hills development, the first of its kind in Tokyo.
G6 1-13-1 Akasaka, Minato-ku 3505–1001 Tameike-sanno

VIRGIN CINEMAS ROPPONGI HILLS

An elegant 9-screen cinema complex offering major blockbuster films, a wide range of art house films, state-of-the-art sound systems, and Japan's largest screen.
F7 Keyakizaka Complex, Roppongi Hills, 6-10-2 Roppongi, Minato-ku 5775–6090 Daily 24 hours Roppongi

WALL STREET BAR

A very popular pub, with a round bar, great bartenders and friendly waitresses. Go late in the evening; very crowded on weekends.
F7 B2 Imperial Roppongi Bldg, 5-16-52 Roppongi, Minato-ku 3586–0874 6pm–8am Roppongi

Restaurants

PRICES

Prices are approximate, based on a 3-course meal for one person.
¥¥¥ over ¥8,000
¥¥ ¥3,000–¥8,000
¥ under ¥3,000

ANDERSEN (¥)
A self-serve deli and sandwich bar in the basement of a bakery. Continental or full breakfasts available.
E7 5-1-26 Aoyama, Minami-Aoyama 3407–4833 Daily 8am–9pm Omotesando

ANNA MILLER'S (¥)
This coffee shop serves American food–Pennsylvania Dutch homemade pies, sandwiches and hamburgers–all night long.
G6 3-5-2 Akasaka, Minato-ku 3586–7369 Daily 24 hours Akasaka

ASENA (¥¥)
Authentic Turkish meze (hors d'oeuvres), kebabs and much more, with a belly-dance show every Friday and Saturday.
G6 Gojuban Building B1, 5-5-11 Akasaka, Minato-ku 3505–5282 Mon–Sat 11–11 Akasaka

ATHARA PETARA (¥)
Classic Sri Lankan fare, including spicy chicken curry with yellow rice and vegetables. Good vegetarian selection.
F7 Ryudocho Building 2F, 7-4-4 Roppongi 3478–3898 Daily 11.30am–5am Nogizaka

BENGAWAN SOLO (¥¥)
Indonesian staff and cooking. The colorful *rijsttafel*, including some highly spiced items, gives you a chance to experience the widest variety of dishes.
F7 Kaneko Building 1F, 7-18-13 Roppongi, Minato-ku 3408–5698 Daily 11.30–3, 5–10 Roppongi

BIKKURI SUSHI (¥)
Patrons help themselves to sushi and *sashami* from a sushi "train." The price varies according to dish color.
F7 3-14-9 Roppongi, Minato-ku 3403–1489 Daily lunch, dinner Roppongi

SOUNDS FAMILIAR

The Japanese have adapted the words as they've adopted the food:
hot dog: *hotto doggu*
hamburger: *hambaga*
sandwich: *sando-itchi*
steak: *suteki*
ham: *hamu*
sausage: *soseji*
salad: *sarada*
bread: *pan*
butter: *bata*
coffee: *kohi*
bacon and egg: *bekon eggu*
orange juice: *orenji jusu*
ice cream: *aisu kurimu*
chocolate cake: *chokoreto keiki*

BINDI (¥)
Tiny counter-style eatery serving home-style Indian food. Delicious onion *pakoda* (onion rings), and *brinjals* (deep-fried eggplant). The 16 different curries provide plenty of choice.
E7 7-10-10 Minami Aoyama, Minato-ku 3409–7114 Daily 11.30–2, 6–10 Omotesando

CAPRICCIOSA (¥)
A cheerful place that serves large portions of pasta and other Mediterranean favorites at fair prices. One of a chain with several branches.
F7 7-13-2 Roppongi, Minato-ku 5410–6061 Daily 11–11 Roppongi

CORIANDER (¥)
The modern Thai cuisine at this ambient late-night restaurant has all the classic Thai flavors.
G8 1-10-6 Nishi-Azabu, Minato-ku 3475–5720 Daily 11–11 Azabu-Juban

FUKUZUSHI (¥¥¥)
Not your usual sushi bar. A chic setting for great sushi in one of the liveliest nighttime areas downtown. This is the chic, expensive end of eating sushi. Unlike most sushi restaurants, this one has a cocktail bar.
F7 5-7-8 Roppongi, Minato-ku 3402–4116 Mon–Sat 11.30–2, 5.30–11 Roppongi

HASSAN (¥¥)
A busy traditional restaurant with seating on chairs or on tatami (straw mats). The set tempura, *sukiyaki* and *shabu-shabu* menus include all-you-can-eat options.
F7 Denki Building B1F, 6-1-20 Roppongi, Minato-ku 3403–8333 Daily 11.30–2, 5–10 Roppongi

JOHNNY ROCKETS (¥)
Good hamburgers, French fries, salads and other fast-food staples.
F7 Coco Roppongi Building 2F, 3-11-10 Roppongi, Minato-ku 3423–1955 Mon–Thu 11–11, Fri–Sat 11am–7am Roppongi

KENBOKKE (¥)
The interior here is modern with few Indian touches, but cuisine of the Bombay-born chef is authentic. Tandoori shirmp and chicken are specialties.
F8 Empire Building 2F, 4-11-28 Nishi-Azabu, Minato-ku 3498–7080 Mon–Sat 11.30–10.30 Hiroo

KUA'AINA (¥)
Well-known for its huge Hawaiian hamburgers and sandwiches.
E7 5-10-21 Minami-Aoyama, Minato-ku 3407–8001 Mon–Sat 11–11.30, Sun and holidays 11–10 Omotesando

MOTI (¥)
An old favorite of locals and expatriates alike. Standard Indian interior and menu, with tasty vegetarian dishes, kormas and chicken masala. This is one of five branches (others include Roppongi).
G6 Kinpa Building 3F, 2-14-31 Akasaka, Minato-ku 3584–6640 Daily 11.30–10 Akasaka

NEWS DELI (¥)
New York-inspired deli fare—salads, soups, sandwiches, pastas and grills. Counter and tables, and take-out service.
E7 SJ Building 1F, 3-6-23 Kita-Aoyama, Minato-ku 3407–1715 Daily 11–11 Omotesando

NOT EXACTLY RAW FISH

Among Westerners, plenty of fallacies exist on the subject of sushi and *sashimi*. "It's raw fish, right?" Not exactly. Morsels of raw fish, shellfish and roes, as well as a few cooked varieties, pressed on to a pad of warm, vinegared rice—that's sushi (or more precisely, *nigirizushi*). Pieces of fish and vegetable rolled in rice and seaweed are *makizushi*. Delicate slices of raw fish and shellfish served with *daikon* (shredded white radish), *wasabi* (green horse-radish paste) and soy sauce—that's *sashimi*, often served as a first course. Sushi can cost from ¥320 a selection to ¥2,400 (and even much more).

NOBU TOKYO (¥¥¥)
Reservations are essential at this classy restaurant where friendly waiters serve contemporary Japanese cuisine with efficiency. Sushi and *sashimi* are on the menu (the sushi rolls are renowned).
H7 4-1-28 Toranomon, Minato-ku 5733–0070 Mon–Fri 11.30–2, daily 6–10 Kamiyacho

SHABUZEN (¥¥)
A big chain restaurant specializing in *shabu-shabu*, and including all-you-can-eat deals.
F7 Aoba Roppongi Building B1, 3-16-33 Roppongi, Minato-ku 3585–5600 Daily 4–11.30 Roppongi

SICILIA (¥)
Popular for pasta, pizza and garden salads, especially on Friday and Saturday.
F7 6-1-26 Roppongi, Minato-ku 3405–4653 Daily lunch, dinner Roppongi

LA VERDE (¥)
Part of a chain, all of which are noted for their large servings of pasta with tasty toppings at low prices. The wines are also good and not expensive.
F6 Aoyama Building B1F, 1-2-3 Kita-Aoyama, Minato-ku 3404–0712 Daily 11–10 Aoyama-Itchome

Chiyoda-ku

This stolid district, the administrative and business center of Tokyo, includes the fine Imperial Palace East Garden, the National Diet Building, the Yasukuni Shrine war memorial and the impressive National Museum of Modern Art.

Sights	54–60
Walk	61
Shopping	62
Entertainment and Nightlife	63
Restaurants	64

Top 25 TOP 25

Imperial Palace East Garden ▷ **54**

Hibiya Park ▷ **56**

National Diet Building ▷ **57**

National Museum of Modern Art ▷ **58**

Yasukuni Shrine ▷ **59**

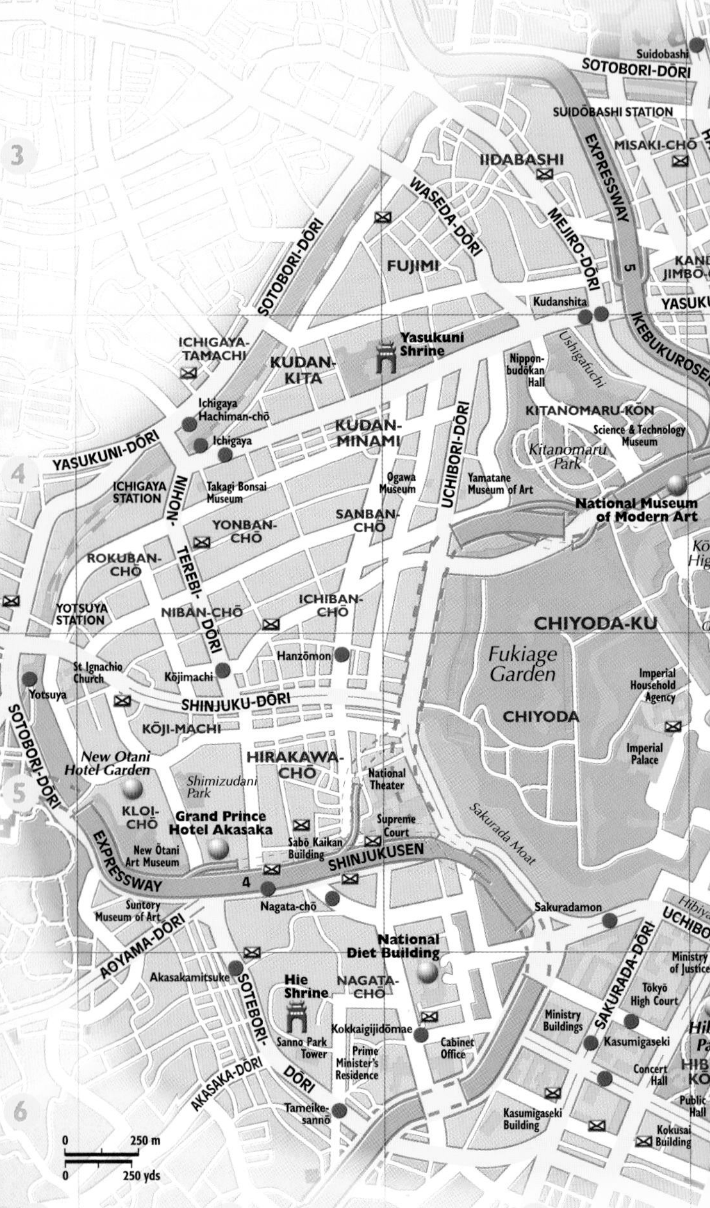
2
3
4
5
6
F
G
H
Suidobashi
SOTOBORI-DŌRI
SUIDŌBASHI STATION
MISAKI-CHŌ
IIDABASHI
EXPRESSWAY
WASEDA-DŌRI
MEJIRO-DŌRI
SOTOBORI-DŌRI
FUJIMI
KANDA
JIMBŌ-C
YASUKU
Kudanshita
5
IKEBUKUROSEN
ICHIGAYA-
TAMACHI
KUDAN-
KITA
Yasukuni
Shrine
Ushigafuchi
Nippon-
budōkan
Hall
Ichigaya
Hachiman-chō
KITANOMARU-KŌN
Science & Technology
Museum
Ichigaya
KUDAN-
MINAMI
UCHIBORI-DŌRI
YASUKUNI-DŌRI
Kitanomaru
Park
ICHIGAYA
STATION
NIHON-
TEREBI-
DŌRI
Takagi Bonsai
Museum
Ogawa
Museum
Yamatane
Museum of Art
National Museum
of Modern Art
YONBAN-
CHŌ
SANBAN-
CHŌ
ROKUBAN-
CHŌ
ICHIBAN-
CHŌ
YOTSUYA
STATION
NIBAN-CHŌ
CHIYODA-KU
Hanzōmon
Fukiage
Garden
St Ignachio
Church
Yotsuya
Kōjimachi
Imperial
Household
Agency
SHINJUKU-DŌRI
KŌJI-MACHI
CHIYODA
Imperial
Palace
New Otani
Hotel Garden
HIRAKAWA-
CHŌ
National
Theater
Shimizudani
Park
KLOI-
CHŌ
Grand Prince
Hotel Akasaka
Supreme
Court
Sakurada Moat
New Ōtani
Art Museum
Sabō Kaikan
Building
SHINJUKUSEN
EXPRESSWAY
4
Suntory
Museum of Art
Nagata-chō
Sakuradamon
Hibiya
UCHIBOR
AOYAMA-DŌRI
National
Diet Building
Ministry
of Justice
Akasakamitsuke
SOTEBORI-
DŌRI
Hie
Shrine
NAGATA-
CHŌ
SAKURADA-DŌRI
Tōkyō
High Court
Ministry
Buildings
Kokkaigijidōmae
Sanno Park
Tower
Cabinet
Office
Kasumigaseki
Prime
Minister's
Residence
Concert
Hall
AKASAKA-DŌRI
Tameike-
sannō
Public
Hall
Kasumigaseki
Building
Kokusai
Building
0
250 m
0
250 yds

HONGŌ-DŌRI
KURAMAEBASHI-DŌRI
SHINOBAZU-DŌRI
Suehiro-chō
SOTO-KANDA
Ochanomizu
OCHANOMIZU STATION
SOTOBORI-DŌRI
SARU-GAKU-CHŌ
KANDA-SURUGADAI
AKIHABARA STATION
Nicolai Cathedral
Shin-ochanomizu
Transportation Museum
Akihabara
Kanda
DŌRI
Jimbō-chō
KANDA SUDA-CHŌ
Iwamotochō
YASUKUNI-DŌRI
Ogawamachi
Awaji-chō
KANDA OGAWA-MACHI
SOTOBORI-DŌRI
KANDAHEISEI-DŌRI
IWAMOTO-CHŌ
Kanda
KANDA NISHIKICHŌ
HONGŌ-DŌRI
KANDA STATION
KANDA KAJI-CHŌ
INNER LOOP EXPRESSWAY
UCHI-KANDA
Takebashi
UCHIBORI-DŌRI
CHŪŌ-DŌRI
Ote Moat
ŌTE-MACHI
Communications Museum
Imperial Palace East Garden
Ōtemachi
Mitsukoshimae
Ōte Center Building
Ōtemachi Building
Nomura Building
Bank of Japan
Money Museum
Ōtemachi
EITAI-DŌRI
HIBIYA-DŌRI
Marunouchi Oazo
Daiichi Tekko Building
SOTOBORI-DŌRI
Tōkyō
TŌKYŌ STATION
International Sightseeing Building
TŌKYO-GAIEN
Marunouchi Building
Nijubashimae
Central Post Office
MARUNOUCHI
Statue of Kusunoki
Shin Tōkyō Building
Idemitsu Museum of Modern Arts
Tōkyō International Forum
Moat
DŌRI
Yūraku-chō
YŪRAKU-CHŌ
Hibiya
YŪRAKU-CHŌ
Mullion
Theater
DŌRI
J
K
L

Imperial Palace East Garden

TOP 25

HIGHLIGHTS

- Otemon (gate)
- Flowering cherry trees
- Sculpted hedges
- Monumental stonework
- Base of old castle keep
- Museum of the imperial collections
- Waterbirds
- Giant carp
- Yells of martial arts students

TIP

- Apply online at http://sankan.kunaicho.go.jp/order/index_EN.html for a tour of the Inner Palace gardens and buildings.

This was once part of the emperor's private garden. Bordered by the massive palace walls, the carefully tended gardens and their water features offer a haven for city workers from the nearby financial district.

Gateway The Imperial Palace East Garden (Higashi Gyoen) is a vast green space in the heart of the city. Once the biggest fortress in the world, the shogun's castle of Edo became the site of the Imperial Palace after 1868. The palace, home to the imperial family, is closed to the public except for two days a year. The usual entrance to the East Garden is through the Otemon, near the Palace Hotel; it was the main castle gate, one of 36 in the outer walls, elaborately designed for defense. If you think you hear the ghosts of warring samurai

People enjoy the Imperial Palace East Garden in various ways, walking, painting, just relaxing; the remains of the old Edo castle keep contrast with the skyscrapers of modern Tokyo beyond the park (bottom, middle right); irises are a stunning feature of the garden in summer (bottom, right)

shouting, it's probably the police martial arts class in the hall next to the guard house. A small museum near the gate shows exhibits from the imperial collections.

The sights A short walk brings you to the massive foundations of the castle keep, crowning a low hill. Notice the perfect fit of the huge stones in the walls: Mortar free, they were designed to withstand earthquakes. There's a good view over the gardens and the city from the top, but imagine the former tower here standing five stories high, and the whole hill densely packed with buildings. The tower was destroyed by fire in 1657 and most of the remaining buildings were razed after the Meiji emperor was restored to power in 1868. There is always something in bloom here, notably azaleas and cherry blossoms in spring and irises in summer.

THE BASICS

J4
3-5-1 Marunouchi, Chiyoda-ku
Tue–Thu, Sat–Sun 9–4 (no entry after 3pm)
Otemachi, Takebashi
Tokyo
Good
Free
More of the Imperial Palace grounds can be seen by special permission; tel 3213–1111, ext 485. Tickets must be collected day before visit. Passports required. Tour times 10–11.30, 1.30–4

Hibiya Park

Pelican fountain (left); locals take a break in the greenery of Hibiya Park (right)

THE BASICS

- J6
- Chiyoda-ku
- 3501–6428
- Daily dawn–11pm
- Good restaurant; snack bars
- Hibiya, Uchisaiwaicho
- Yurakucho
- Good
- Free

HIGHLIGHTS

- Bonsai shop
- Ponds and fountains
- Floral borders all year
- Outdoor concerts
- Imperial Hotel, opposite
- Intricate trellises
- Hibiya City–winter skating

TIP

- On many weekends Japanese and international festivals take place in the park.

In this tranquil corner of the city, Tokyo's first public park, secretaries from nearby offices eat their box lunches, lovers can find private retreats, and tired tourists rest up from sightseeing.

In the park The 6 acres (2.5ha) of Hibiya Park form a green extension to the Imperial Palace Outer Garden. On one side of Hibiya Park are the ministry buildings of Kasumigaseki, the edge of Ginza is only a block away on the other. In the park itself fountains play, waterbirds swim on the ponds and gardeners groom the flowerbeds and trim the trees into impeccable order. The constructions of rope and wood they build to support precious specimens through the winter snows are works of art. There are public tennis courts, a shop that sells bonsai trees, and on weekend afternoons occasional pop and rock concerts in the outdoor auditorium. Mostly though, people come to stroll and sit, away from crowds and traffic. Visitors from out of town always like to be photographed here.

The vicinity Facing the southeast side of the park is the massive Imperial Hotel (1970), which replaced Frank Lloyd Wright's 1920s original, torn down in 1967. The new hotel's vast lobby is one of Tokyo's favorite meeting points. Nearby Hibiya City, an office building and shopping complex, is modeled after New York's Rockefeller Plaza, with an outdoor skating rink in winter. Across the Harumi-dori from the Imperial Hotel is the Dai-Ichi building–once General MacArthur's headquarters.

The design of Japan's parliament building was much debated during its construction

National Diet Building

This art deco building, capped by a stepped pyramid, houses Japan's national legislature and is opulent inside. Sessions—which you can watch from the public gallery or on closed-circuit TV—can be lively or tedious.

The building A competition was held in 1918 for designs for a new Imperial Diet Building (Kokkaigijido); work started in 1920 and took 16 years to finish. Japanese militarism was growing at the time, and the last thing the generals who controlled the government wanted was a genuine parliament. Many politicians then became involved in the debate over what the final building should look like and whether the building should be Japanese or Western in style and by a Japanese or a foreign architect. When the odd-looking building finally opened, the Imperial Diet had become no more than a rubber stamp. Not until 1946 was there the first general election with universal suffrage, with women finally gaining the vote. The following year the new National Diet met, replacing the old Imperial Diet.

Visits When the Diet is in session you can sit in the public gallery of either house. You need your passports and, for some sessions, a letter of introduction from your embassy. Admission is by token, which you can get at the office on the north side of the building. Organized tours take you into the House of Representatives, the House of Councillors (when the Diet is not in session) and a selection of other rooms.

THE BASICS

www.sangiin.go.jp/eng
H6
1-7-1 Nagatacho, Chiyoda-ku
5521–7445
Mon–Fri 8–5; closed national holidays and Dec 27–Jan 3
Snack bar
Kokkaigijido-mae, Nagatacho
Good Free
Guided tours include the Emperor's Room, Imperial Family's Room, Central Hall and Front Courtyard. Carry your passport

HIGHLIGHTS

- **Marble halls and bronze doors**
- **Imperial throne**
- **Stained-glass ceilings**
- **Lacquer and mother-of-pearl decoration**

TIP

- **If you'd like to take a tour, arrive early; individuals are advised to visit after 9am.**

National Museum of Modern Art

Museum exterior (left); Seven Prayers *by Kentaro Kimura (middle);* Idea of an Image *by Marini Marino (right)*

THE BASICS

www.momat.go.jp/english/index.html
H4
3-1 Kitanomaru Koen, Chiyoda-ku
3214–2561
Tue–Sun 10–5 (also Fri in summer until 8); closed Tue if Mon a national holiday and Dec 28–Jan 1
Takebashi
Good
Moderate

HIGHLIGHTS

- *Ascension*, Tatsuoki Nambata
- Portrait of Alma Mahler, Kokoschka
- *Deep Woods*, Keigetsu Matsubayashi
- *Bathing*, Taketaro Shinkai
- *Stream*, bronze nude by Taimu Tatehata

TIP

- The museum is a three-minute walk from Takebashi station.

The best of 20th-century painting by Japanese artists, many of them influenced by the West, is exhibited side by side with major works by their European contemporaries.

The museum The National Museum of Modern Art (Kokuritsu Kindai Bijutsukan) is in Kitanomaru Park, formerly a part of the Imperial Palace gardens. The severe concrete box of a building was designed by Yoshiro Taniguchi and built in 1969. Inside, the galleries are spacious and skillfully lit. The ground floor houses temporary exhibitions, the top three the permanent collection. Many foreign visitors are initially drawn to the familiar work of Klee and Chagall, and the fine portrait of Alma Mahler by Kokoschka, and then turn to works of Japanese painters who worked in France and Germany early in the 20th century. Tetsugoro Yorozu's nudes might almost be by Matisse, and Tsuguharu Fujita was practically an honorary Frenchman. Some of the most ravishing pictures are by those who developed the Japanese idiom in new ways—as in Kanzan Shimomura's luminous *Autumn Among Trees*, Gyokudo Kawai's 12-panel *Parting Spring* and Shinsui Ito's *Snowy Evening*.

Crafts gallery Just across Kitanomaru Park is an impressive brick building of 1910—once headquarters of the Imperial Guard. It now houses exhibitions of 20th-century craft work, including fine textiles, graphic design, ceramics, lacquer-work and metal-work, both traditional and modern.

White doves at Yasukuni shrine (left); visitors come to honor the war dead (right)

Yasukuni Shrine

Japan's war dead are remembered at this most important of Shinto shrines. The adjacent War Memorial Museum, Yushukan, honors those killed in action and includes a suicide plane, military memorabilia and weaponry.

Spirits and sacrifices Yasukuni shrine on Kudan Hill, northwest of the Imperial Palace, was founded on the orders of Emperor Meiji in 1869 for the worship of the spirits, the *mitama*, of those who had sacrificed their lives in the battles for the restoration the previous year. Now the shrine honors the 2.5 million who died "in the defense of the empire" in the years that followed, although it is controversial because these deaths mainly occurred in aggressive wars in China, the Pacific and Southeast Asia. Flocks of white doves live in the grounds of the shrine.

Instruments of destruction The museum commemorates the Russo-Japanese War of 1905, the invasion of Manchuria and World War II. Exhibits range from samurai armor and swords to 20th-century guns, tanks and planes, including a carrier-borne bomber and a replica Oka, a kamikaze rocket-powered winged bomb. Particularly moving are the thousands of photographs of young people who died during World War II. Newsreels of the last days of World War II show fleets of B-29s showering bombs on Japan, kamikaze pilots taking off on their one-way missions, the devastation caused by the atomic bombs, and the emperor's surrender speech in August 1945.

THE BASICS

www.yasukuni.or.jp
H4
3-1-1 Kudankita, Chiyoda-ku
Museum: 3261–8326
Shrine daily dawn–dusk. Museum daily 9–5 (last admission 4.30); closed Jun 22–23, Dec 28–31
Café
Kudanshita (Exit A1)
Good
Shrine free. Museum inexpensive

HIGHLIGHTS

- *Torii* weighing 100 tons
- Flocks of white doves
- Japanese garden
- Samurai weapons
- Mitsubishi Zero
- Man-guided torpedo
- Tributes to fallen heroes
- Historic newsreels
- War campaign timelines

TIP

- Yasakuni shrine is about a four-minute walk from Kudanshita station.

More to See

GRAND PRINCE HOTEL AKASAKA

The hotel stands on a central hilltop site, so the bar and restaurant on the top of its 40 stories have the city's best view of Akasaka, the Imperial Palace, Ginza and Tokyo Bay.

G5 1-2 Kioicho, Chiyoda-ku 3234–1111 Daily 11.30am–midnight Bar and restaurants Nagatacho

HIE SHRINE

One of Tokyo's most picturesque shrines is opposite the main entrance to the Capitol Tokyu Hotel. You will notice statues of monkeys carrying their young: One of the deities enshrined here is believed to protect women against miscarriages. Hie shrine was a favorite of the shoguns and the site of Edo's greatest religious festival.

G6 2-10-5 Nagatacho, Chiyoda-ku 3581–2471 Daily dawn–dusk Kokkaigijido-mae Free

IDEMITSU MUSEUM OF MODERN ARTS

The Asian art on display here–including calligraphy, paintings and ceramics–is superb. Two 16th-century screens–one of cherry blossoms, the other of colorful kimonos–show that Japanese reverence for these subjects is nothing new. The collection is so vast that only a tiny fraction can be seen at one time. One room is devoted to an archive of pot shards of the world. Check out the great view of central Tokyo from the windows.

J5 9th floor, Kokusai Building, 3-1-1 Marunouchi, Chyoda-ku 5777–8600 Tue–Sun 10–5; closed Dec 29–Jan 3 Free tea Yurakucho Moderate

NEW OTANI HOTEL GARDEN

Next to the giant hotel is a fine traditional Japanese garden with streams and lily ponds, decorative bridges and manicured shrubs. It continues the tradition of an early Edo-period garden on this site.

G5 4-1 Kioicho, Chiyoda-ku 3265–1111 Daily 9–9 In hotel Yotsuya Moderate (free for hotel guests)

Festival dress at the Hie shrine

View of the New Otani Hotel Garden

Imperial Palace East Garden to Hibiya Park

This walk takes in two of Tokyo's finest parks and gardens, the Imperial Palace East Garden and the Western-inspired Hibiya Park.

DISTANCE: 1 mile (1.5km) **ALLOW:** 3 hours

START

IMPERIAL PALACE EAST GARDEN
J5 Tokyo

END

HIBIYA PARK
J6 Hibiya

❶ The East Garden of the Imperial Palace (▷ 54) is set on the site of the former Edo castle. Make a dramatic entry to the garden through the Otemon, the main castle gate.

❷ **Inside the garden, you'll see the huge stone castle walls and can enjoy a stroll around a classic Japanese formal garden.**

❸ Check out the small museum housing the art collection of Emperor Showa. Open 9–4.30 (but subject to times of the year).

❹ **Leaving the garden behind, walk 545 yards (500m) southward down Uchibori-dori, adjacent to the palace moat, to arrive in Wadakura Square.**

❺ Pause to admire the square's fascinating sculptural fountains.

❻ **Another 545-yard (500m) walk takes you past the broad Imperial Palace Plaza. Stop here to get a feel for some rare Tokyo open space. You may be lucky and see the mounted police in their colorful uniforms.**

❼ A final 545-yard (500m) walk brings you to Hibiya Park. Once part of the Imperial Palace grounds, and redesigned in the 19th century in the Western style, the paths and ponds combine the best of European and Eastern garden design.

❽ **Take some time to explore Hibiya Park (▷ 56), just a stone's throw from Ginza and a popular place for workers to take their lunch break.**

Shopping

AKIHABARA
www.akiba.or.jp/english/index.html
Several blocks of multi-story emporia are stuffed with everything from electronic marvels to workaday washing machines. Smaller stores specialize in computer software, mobile phones, anime products and video games. Carry your passport for duty-free concessions, and don't be afraid to ask for discounts.
K3 Akihabara Akihabara

BIC CAMERA
Eight floors of the latest electronic gear. Be sure to get an English manual and make sure it runs on the correct voltage.
J6 1-11-1 Yurakucho, Chiyoda-ku 5221-1112 Daily 10–8 Yurakucho

ISHIMARU DENKI
A great range of electronic products that can be used overseas–check out the range of amazing high-tech Japanese toilet seats.
K3 1-15-4 Sotokanda, Chiyoda-ku 3255-1600 Daily 10–8 Akihabara

ISSEIDO
Secondhand books, art books and attractive woodblock prints.
J3 1-7 Kanda-Jimbocho, Chiyoda-ku 3292-0071 Daily 10–4 Jimbocho

KANDA-JIMBOCHO
An area with many secondhand bookshops stocking Japanese and foreign books and woodblock prints.
J3 Jimbocho

LAOX
This giant electrical retailer has four buildings in Akihabara. The duty-free branch is nearby at 1-13-3 Soto-Kanda.
K3 1-2-9 Soto-Kanda, Chiyoda-ku 3253-7111 Mon–Sat 10–7.45, Sun 10–7.15 Akihabara

MINAMI MUSEN
Five floors are packed with all kinds of electrical equipment. The 7th floor houses imported furniture, including a range of antiques.
K3 4-3-3 Soto-Kanda, Chiyoda-ku 3255-3730 Daily 9–5.30 Akihabara

COLLECTIBLE ANTIQUES

Antiques (which in Japan are anything more than about 50 years old), are generally expensive. Fine pieces fetch enormous sums, although the market has settled down since the 1980s boom. Specifically, Japanese collectibles include ceramics, dolls, swords, lacquerware, masks, netsuke–a small and often intricately carved toggle of ivory or wood, used to fasten a small container to a kimono sash–paintings, woodcarvings and woodblock prints.

OHYA-SHOBO
Among several secondhand book and print shops clustered along the road heading east from the station, this one has a vast stock of antique books and fine prints.
J3 1-1 Kanda-Jimbocho, Chiyoda-ku 3291-0062 Mon–Sat 10–6.30 Jimbocho

TOKYO ANIME CENTER
Colorful anime characters hang in the windows. Filled with anime products and information, both Japanese and English.
K3 Akihabara UDX 4F, 4-14-1 Soto-Kanda, Chiyoda-ku 5298-1188 Daily 11–7 Akihabara

YAMAGIWA
This store specializes in lighting fixtures and sells everything from light bulbs to satellite dishes. You'll find both domestic and imported lines.
K3 1-5-10 Soto-Kanda, Chiyoda-ku 3253-5111 Mon–Fri 11.30–7.30, Sat–Sun 11–7.30 Akihabara

YODOBASHI-AKIBA
A huge electronics store right in the middle of Akihabara. Browse to your heart's content on nine floors with more than 600,000 items.
K3 1-1 Kanda-Hanaokacho, Chiyoda-ku 3632-1010 Daily 9.30–9 Akihabara

Entertainment and Nightlife

AKASAKA

Two parallel streets, Hitotsugi-dori and Tamachi-dori, and the narrow alleyways between them are packed with bars, clubs and restaurants. It's respectable and rather expensive, although not quite in the Ginza league, and mostly frequented by company men on expense accounts and people staying at the area's big hotels.

AKASAKA ACT THEATER

A comfortable medium-size theater (seating for 1,236)–which presents drama, dance, music (including musicals) and concerts.

G6 ✉ 5-3-6 Akasaka, Akasaka ☎ 5561–0909 Daily 7pm–11pm Moderate to expensive Akasaka

CHANTER CINE

A multiscreen cinema complex, with three halls, featuring mainly European and American films, but also showcases fine films from Africa, Asia and the Middle East.

J6 ✉ 1-2-2 Yurakucho, Chiyoda-ku ☎ 3591–1511 Moderate Hibiya

KUDAN KAIKAN BEER GARDEN

A popular Japanese rooftop beer garden open in the warmer weather, from about mid-May to late September.

H3 ✉ 1-6-5 Kudan-Minami, Chiyoda-ku ☎ 3261–5521 Mon–Fri 5–10, Sat–Sun and public holidays 5–9 Kudanshita

NATIONAL THEATER (KOKURITSU GEKIJO)

Kokuritsu Gekijo, the only classical art theater of Japan, features kabuki and the *hogaku* (traditional Japanese music) in the Large Theater and *gagaku*, and *bunraku* (▷ below) in its Small Theater. The Engei Hall offers *rakugo,* a form of sit-down comedy, *manzai*, a form of stand-up comedy, and *kodan*, or storytelling. There are authentic displays of traditional Japanese art in the exhibition rooms. The beautiful building was built to resemble the Todaiji Temple in Nara.

G5 ✉ 4-1 Hayabusacho, Chiyoda-ku ☎ 3265–7411 Expensive Hanzomon

BUNRAKU

In this form of theater, three puppeteers work near-lifesize figures, while narrators tell the stories to a musical accompaniment. The stories told are similar to kabuki and the scripts traditional and usually well known by the audience. Like noh, it is an esoteric art for which few foreigners acquire a taste. Performances are sometimes staged at the small hall of the National Theater (▷ above).

NIPPON BUDOKAN HALL

The martial arts arena built for the 1964 Olympics. Matches and courses are held almost continuously here and visitors are welcome to come and watch.

H3 ✉ 2-3 Kitanomaru Koen, Chiyoda-ku ☎ 3216–5100 Kudanshita

TOKYO ANIME CENTER

www.animecenter.jp

The center's Event Gallery hosts a variety of anime-related events and its AKIBA3D Theater conducts regular screenings of popular visuals and previews of the latest. Through a glass panel, you can watch voice actors recording scenes in the recording studio. Check the website for what's on.

K3 ✉ Akihabara UDX 4F, 4-14-1 Soto-Kanda, Chiyoda-ku ☎ 5298–1188 Daily 11–7 Moderate Akihabara

TOKYO TAKARAZUKA THEATER

http://kageki.hankyu.co.jp/english/index.html

The Takarazuka Revue Company is a famous all-female variety troupe. Performances are usually romantic love stories, and the audience is mostly female. Shows are very popular, so book early.

J6 ✉ 1-1-3 Yurakucho, Chiyoda-ku ☎ 5251–2001 Daily 11–5 Moderate to expensive Hibiya

Restaurants

PRICES

Prices are approximate, based on a 3-course meal for one person.

¥¥¥	over ¥8,000
¥¥	¥3,000–¥8,000
¥	under ¥3,000

AJANTA (¥)
An old favorite, with the simplest of settings but one of the most comprehensive menus in Tokyo. The southern and northern Indian dishes are as authentic as you will find.
G5 3-11 Nibancho, Chiyoda-ku 3264–4255 Daily 24 hours Kojimachi

CLUB NYX (¥¥)
French country-style cooking, and Parisian decor make this licensed restaurant popular with French expats and visitors, but it is much adored by the locals. Lunch is served until 2.30, but you can buy delicious crusty galettes all afternoon.
J6 2-6-16 Ginza, Chuo-ku 5524–3939 Daily 11.45–9.30 Hibiya

DENPACHI (¥¥)
This popular evening-only diner, with its minimal furnishings, specializes in sardine dishes. But a range of beef tongue dishes and Okinawan-style stir-fried *soba* with *mentaiko* make for some interesting variety.
J6 4-8-7 Ginza, Chuo-ku 3562-3957 Daily 4.30–10.25 Ginza

ROBATA (¥)
Old-style wooden restaurant serving authentic Japanese country cuisine. Dishes are placed on a circular wooden counter, one by one, and include vegetable stews, tofu dishes and pork mains.
J6 1-3-8 Yurakucho, Chiyoda-ku 3591–1905 Mon–Sat 5–10.30 Hibiya

ROSSO E NERO (¥¥)
A good choice if you want a change from traditional Japanese fare. Here you will find home cooking, with good antipasti, a wide variety of pastas, sauces and grills. The menu includes some filling Austrian fare as well as Italian dishes, notably the fruit strudel and dumpling desserts.
G5 Kioicho Building 2F, 3-12 Kioicho, Chiyoda-ku 3237–5888 Daily 11.30–2, 5.30–9 Nagatacho

MISO SOUP

Miso is a popular soup served with meals, including breakfast. Its base is a fish stock, made from the bonito, which is sold in dried flakes in every food store in Japan. This stock is then seasoned with miso paste. Floating in the soup are small squares of tofu and strands of seaweed or finely chopped vegetables. In the Japanese manner, the soup is slurped with gusto from the bowl while the solid bits are held back with the chopsticks.

TOKYO JOE'S (¥¥)
Come here for volume and value. The most popular dish is the butter and mustard stone crab. These crabs are flown in fresh from the Florida Keys.
G6 Akasaka Eight-One Building, B1, 2-13-5 Nagatacho, Chiyoda-ku 3508–0325 Daily 11.30–3, 5–11.30 Akasaka-Mitsuke

TSUKI NO SHIZUKU (¥¥¥)
A tasteful decor of running water and rock gardens, little footbridges and bamboo blinds divide small dining rooms. The menu features lots of tofu and yuba dishes, plus grilled pork and chicken dishes.
J6 3-1 Ginza, Chuo-ku 5159–0250 Daily 11.30–2, 4–11 Ginza

YABU SOBA (¥)
One of Tokyo's most famous *soba* shops, in an old Japanese house, decked with *shoji* screens and woodblock prints. It is so popular you may have quite a wait to get served.
K4 2-10 Kanda-Awajicho, Chiyoda-ku 3251–0287 Daily 11.30–7.30 Awajicho

Ginza is the flashy, chic heart of Tokyo and while it might not be your first choice as a shopping district, walk the streets and window shop for some of the world's finest merchandise.

Sights	68–76
Walk	77
Shopping	78
Entertainment and Nightlife	79–80
Restaurants	81–82

Top 25 TOP 25

Ginza ▷ **68**

Hamarikyu Garden and River Cruise ▷ **70**

Kabuki-za Theater ▷ **72**

Sony Building ▷ **73**

Tokyo Tower ▷ **74**

Tsukiji Fish Market ▷ **75**

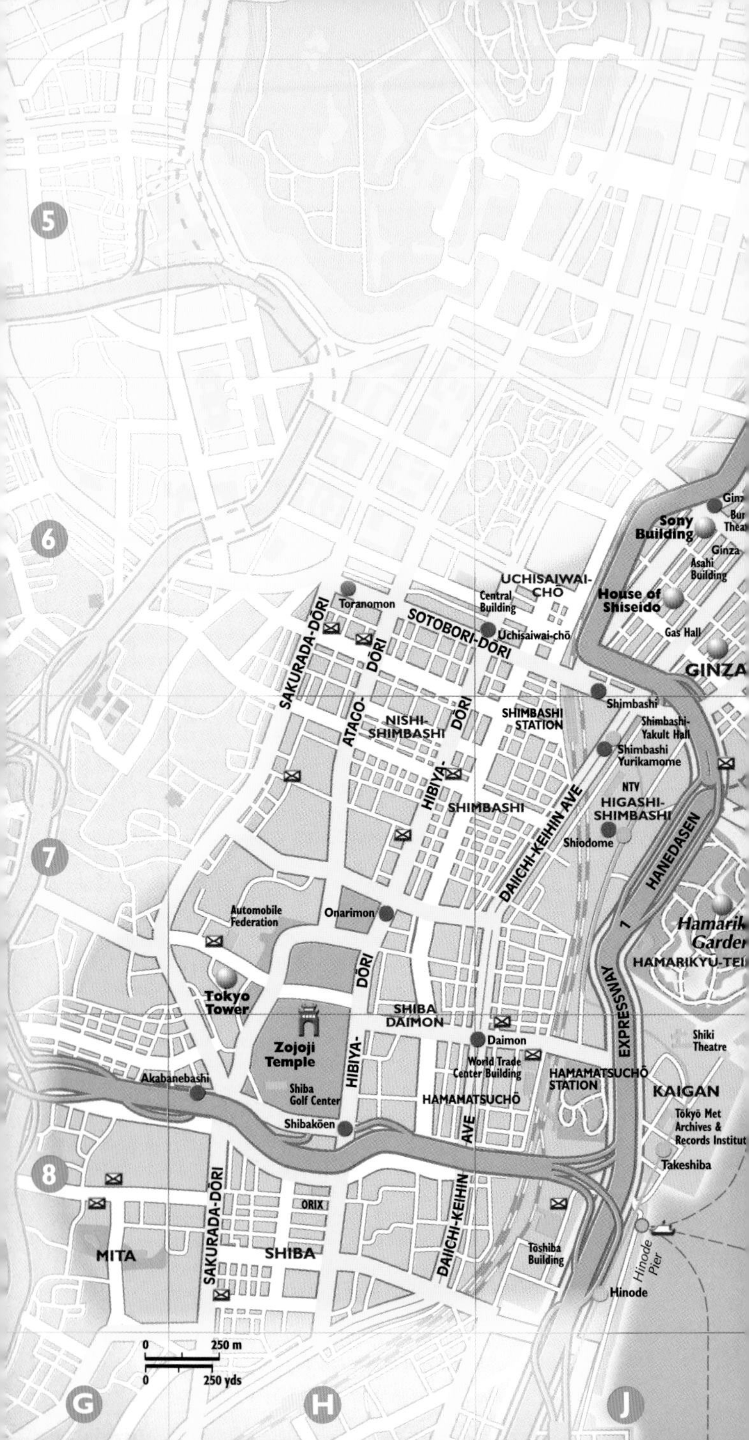

5
6
7
8
G
H
J
UCHISAIWAI-CHŌ
Central Building
Toranomon
SOTOBORI-DŌRI
Uchisaiwai-chō
SAKURADA-DŌRI
ATAGO-DŌRI
NISHI-SHIMBASHI
HIBIYA-DŌRI
SHIMBASHI STATION
Shimbashi
Shimbashi-Yakult Hall
Shimbashi Yurikamome
NTV
HIGASHI-SHIMBASHI
Shiodome
SHIMBASHI
DAIICHI-KEIHIN AVE
HANEDASEN
Sony Building
Ginza
Asahi Building
House of Shiseido
Gas Hall
GINZA
Automobile Federation
Onarimon
Tokyo Tower
Zojoji Temple
Shiba Golf Center
SHIBA DAIMON
Daimon
World Trade Center Building
HAMAMATSUCHŌ STATION
HAMAMATSUCHŌ
HIBIYA-
AVE
EXPRESSWAY
1
HAMARIKYU-TEI
Shiki Theatre
KAIGAN
Tōkyō Met Archives & Records Institut
Takeshiba
Akabanebashi
Shibakōen
SAKURADA-DŌRI
ORIX
MITA
SHIBA
DAIICHI-KEIHIN
Toshiba Building
Hinode
Hinode Pier
0 250 m
0 250 yds

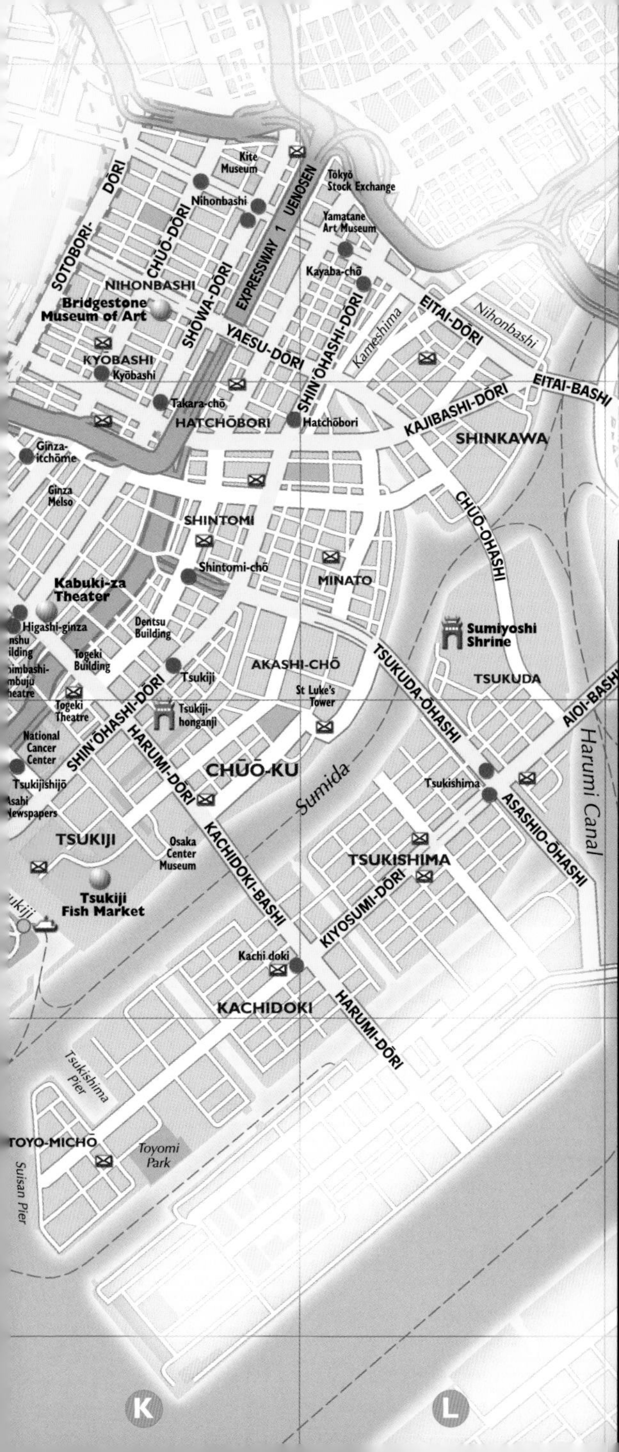

Around Ginza

Kite Museum
Tōkyō Stock Exchange
DŌRI
Nihonbashi
EXPRESSWAY 1 UENOSEN
Yamatane Art Museum
SOTOBORI-
CHŪŌ-DŌRI
Kayaba-chō
NIHONBASHI
Bridgestone Museum of Art
SHŌWA-DŌRI
SHIN'ŌHASHI-DŌRI
Kameshima
EITAI-DŌRI
Nihonbashi
YAESU-DŌRI
KYŌBASHI
Kyōbashi
EITAI-BASHI
KAJIBASHI-DŌRI
Takara-chō
HATCHŌBORI
Hatchōbori
SHINKAWA
Ginza-itchōme
Ginza Melso
CHŪŌ-ŌHASHI
SHINTOMI
Shintomi-chō
MINATO
Kabuki-za Theater
Higashi-ginza
Dentsu Building
Sumiyoshi Shrine
Togeki Building
AKASHI-CHŌ
TSUKUDA-ŌHASHI
TSUKUDA
Tsukiji
St Luke's Tower
AIOI-BASHI
Togeki Theatre
SHIN'ŌHASHI-DŌRI
Tsukiji-honganji
Harumi Canal
National Cancer Center
HARUMI-DŌRI
CHŪŌ-KU
Sumida
Tsukishima
Tsukijishijō
ASASHIO-ŌHASHI
TSUKIJI
Osaka Center Museum
KACHIDOKI-BASHI
TSUKISHIMA
KIYOSUMI-DŌRI
Tsukiji Fish Market
Kachi doki
KACHIDOKI
HARUMI-DŌRI
Tsukishima Pier
TOYO-MICHŌ
Toyomi Park
Suisan Pier
K
L

Ginza

TOP 25

HIGHLIGHTS

- Ginza 4-chome crossing
- Lights of Ginza by night
- Wako's elegant displays
- Basement food departments
- Mikimoto pearl shop
- Beer halls
- Side street discount shops
- Sunday strolling on Chuo-dori

TIP

- Look out for quality goods marked down in the department stores.

The Ginza neighborhood has the most expensive real estate on earth, and its stores and clubs have prices to match. On a par with New York's Fifth Avenue, you can browse elegant stores alongside Toyko's wealthiest citizens.

Stores The name Ginza derives from the silver mint that the shogun built in the area in 1612. Money attracts money, and merchants soon set up shops nearby. Their successors are the famous department stores of today, two of which—Wako and Mitsukoshi—stand at the heart of Ginza, the "Yon-chome" (4-chome). This is at the intersection of two main streets, Harumi-dori and Chuo-dori. On Sunday afternoons the latter is closed to vehicles; when the weather is fine, cafés put out tables and umbrellas. Prices are high in most

Dramatic entrance to Ginza's Kabuki-za Theater (far left); busy Yon-chome (top middle); shopping on a grand scale on the Yon-chome (top right); shop window displays (bottom left and right); a tempting bakery (bottom middle)

stores. But not all the shopping is on a grand scale. Down the side streets, you can find boutiques and little specialty stores where prices are almost reasonable, along with hostess clubs and bars where they are outrageous. Restaurants can be extraordinarily expensive, too, but you can find something sensibly priced at one of the department stores, and in side streets.

Sights Although many buildings today are steel-and-glass and have neon signs, several late 19th-century buildings survive, including the Wako store with a famous landmark clock tower. Down Harumi-dori near Higashi-Ginza subway station is the rebuilt Kabuki-za Theater (▷ 72) with matinee and evening performances on most days. Continue in the same direction and you will reach Tsukiji Fish Market (▷ 75) and the Sumida River.

THE BASICS

J6

Chuo-ku

Countless restaurants and fast-food outlets

Ginza, Higashi-Ginza

Yurakucho

Few

Free

Hamarikyu Garden and River Cruise

HIGHLIGHTS

- River views
- Duck lakes
- Seawater tidal pond
- Causeway bridges
- Teahouse
- Japanese formal garden
- Peony garden
- Flowering trees, all year
- Precious trees wrapped up for winter
- River cruises

TIP

- Book a place at a tea ceremony in the teahouse.

The scene at this tranquil 62-acre (25ha) garden can have changed little since feudal lords came duck hunting here. Ponds, planted thickly with reeds and bamboo, provide cover for the hundreds of waterfowl.

The garden Now hemmed in between an expressway and the Sumida River, the Hamarikyu Garden, also known as Hama Detached Palace Garden, was once part of the private game reserve of the Tokugawa shoguns and comprises water, woods and gardens. Clever planting ensures that some species are always in bloom, and big areas are much less formal than in the typical Japanese garden. The river is tidal here, and seawater flows in and out of one of the ponds. Long causeway bridges with wisteria-

A bridge over the lake in Hamarikyu Garden (top left); a colorful display of flowers (top right); the enchanting Nakajima teahouse (bottom left); tea and a sweet delicacy served in the teahouse (bottom middle); people taking tea (bottom right)

covered trellises lead across the river to a replica of the picturesque Nakajima teahouse where Emperor Meiji entertained President Ulysses S. Grant and Mrs. Grant in 1879. The 300-year-old pine tree near the entrance was planted by one of the early shoguns.

River boats Apart from the pleasure of strolling, the best reason for a visit is to catch one of the water buses for a cruise upriver to the area of Asakusa, with its temple and small shops (▷ 86). Boats leave the eastern tip of the garden every half-hour or so, for a 45-minute trip that gives you a completely different view of Tokyo. Nearby Hinoda Pier—a five-minute walk from Hamamatsucho station—is the terminus for other Tokyo Bay cruises including those to Shinagawa Aquarium and Odaiba (▷ 100).

THE BASICS

- J7
- 1-1 Hamarikyuteien, Chuo-ku
- 3541–0200
- Tue–Sun 9–4.30; closed Dec 29–Jan 3
- Shimbashi, Higashi-Ginza, Shiodome
- Good
- Moderate

Kabuki-za Theater

Entrance to the theater (left); dramatic posters displayed outside the theater (right)

THE BASICS

www.shochiku.co.jp/play/kabukiza/theater
K6
4-12-15 Ginza, Chuo-ku
3541–3131
Daily 10–6 (box office)
Restaurants and food stalls
Higashi-Ginza, A3 exit
Fair
Expensive

HIGHLIGHTS

- Traditional "shamisen" music
- Magnificent costumes
- Spectacular stage settings
- Dramatic makeup
- Tragic tales

TIP

- For a one-act ticket, be sure to arrive at the box office early.

A visit to the Kabuki-za Theater is a memorable cultural experience. Be sure to rent an audioguide in English to fully appreciate the story and tradition behind the dramatic music, vivid costumes and fantastic settings.

Quite a performance This distinctive Ginza landmark, with its big hanging lanterns and posters, was first opened in 1889. The building was destroyed in 1921 by fire and was rebuilt in the style of 16th-century Japanese castles. It was destroyed by bombs during World War II, but was again rebuilt and is now one of Tokyo's finest examples of Meiji-era architecture. A full kabuki performance can last four to five hours, including two intermissions, and tickets cost upward of ¥2,500 (¥15,000 for good seats). You can rent an English-language "Earphone Guide" that provides commentary on the plot, the actors, the music and kabuki generally. And an English program is invaluable.

You can also opt for one act of the play, for about ¥1,000, which can be up to 90 minutes long. You must stand in line for 30 minutes for the one-act seats and tickets for the full program can be ordered by phone or at the box office.

Refreshment breaks During the intermissions you can enjoy *oden*, *soba*, tempura or sushi in one of the theater's five Japanese-style restaurants. Sandwiches and drinks are also available at food stalls, and there are colorful kabuki dolls and gifts on sale in the souvenir shop.

A Global Positioning System (GPS) on display (left); high-tech recorders for sale (right)

Sony Building

Here six floors of electronic marvels are set up for hands-on testing. There's always a queue of eager people waiting to try out the latest PlayStation.

Showroom Japan leads the world in consumer electronics, launching an endless succession of innovations. Sony—one of the biggest companies and the one that put "Walkman" into the world's dictionaries—is in the forefront, and this center in Ginza is its shop window. Here you can not only see new products but also try them out. Miniaturization is a specialty and you'll see tiny cellular phones, personal CD players, minicams and DVD recorders. Positioning equipment using earth satellites was top secret not so many years ago; now there are simple hand-held models that will tell you accurately where on earth you are and mark the spot on a map.

Demonstrations Now that everyone has a television, the industry has to produce something better and the marketing wizards have to persuade people to buy it. High definition television (HDTV) is already here; you can see its brilliantly crisp pictures on a huge screen. Check out the Air Board, a cordless, hand-held flat screen that uses wireless technology for portable viewing. Try the latest laptop computers with their built-in digital cameras and microphones that transmit your image and voice to other computers. Other tenants in the building include BMW, clothing shops and a good selection of Japanese restaurants.

THE BASICS

www.sonybuilding.jp/e/
J6
5-3-1 Ginza, Chuo-ku
3573–2371
Daily 11–7; closed Jan 1
Cafés on several levels; restaurants in same building
Ginza
Yurakucho
Few
Free

HIGHLIGHTS

- Super-realistic video games
- Big screen HDTV
- Tiny Walkmans and DVDs
- Minidiscs
- Digital cameras
- Global positioning
- PlayStation
- Entertainment robots

TIP

- Do your research here before you go on to purchase any electronics.

Tokyo Tower

A striking view of the Tokyo Tower (left); the observation deck on a clear day (right)

THE BASICS

www.tokyotower.co.jp
H7
4-2-8 Shiba Koen, Minato-ku
3433–5111
Daily 9am–10pm
Snack bars and cafés
Kamiyacho, Onarimon
Good (access possible to first level)
Expensive

HIGHLIGHTS

- Observation decks at 492ft and 820ft (150m and 250m)
- View from 820ft (250m) at night
- View of Mount Fuji (1 day in 5)
- Tokyo Tower Trick Art Gallery
- Aquarium
- Hologram exhibition

TIP

- Avoid daytime crowds and visit at night for spectacular city views.

Tokyo's answer to the Eiffel Tower exceeds the original in height by 30ft (13m). Come on a clear day for a fine view of the Sumida River and Tokyo Bay, Ginza and the Imperial Palace.

The tower At Kamiyacho subway station, emerge from Exit 1 and head uphill. It takes about seven minutes to walk to the foot of the tower. Built in 1958 to carry television transmissions, it now broadcasts all Tokyo's channels as well as FM radio stations. Cameras at the 1,093-ft (333m) level keep an eye on the city's notorious traffic and send pictures to a central control room, which is the source of the information flashed up along the expressways. The tower is the world's tallest freestanding iron structure. The view from the 492-ft (150m) main observatory gives you a 360-degree view of the surrounding Kanto region. Afterward, relax with a cup of coffee at the Café La Tour, then visit the Shinto shrine and "Goods Store" on the next floor. You need to pay extra to go to 820ft (250m) where the view is excellent on a clear day.

The extras The attractions around the base and lower levels are all expensive. An aquarium, on the first floor, holds 50,000 fish of some 800 varieties, and its shop sells many colorful species. On the fourth floor is the Trick Art Gallery where 3-D pictures are painted in special paints to create unusual effects. The third floor has a wax museum and a hologram exhibition with some stunning and interesting works.

A must for fish lovers, Tsukiji Fish Market is always a colorful and lively experience

TOP 25

Tsukiji Fish Market

Even though the famed early-morning tuna auctions are now not open to visitors, the world's largest fish market is still an amazing spectacle, with its mind-boggling array of fish and hive of frenetic activity.

The auctions Since the Japanese are particular about their sushi and *sashimi*, seafood has to reach the consumer in perfect condition. An enormous industry ensures that it does, and 90 percent of the fish eaten in Tokyo passes through Tsukiji Fish Market in the Central Wholesale Market. The action begins at 5am, when buyers inspect the giant bluefin tuna, smaller yellowfin and aptly named "big eyes," flown in fresh from all over the world. Visitors are not permitted at the auctions, but there is still plenty to see from the sidelines as the huge tunas are wheeled away to awaiting vans.

The market In the neighboring wholesale market, 1,200 stalls sell every sort of fish and crustacean, many of them still jumping or crawling. Buyers for the city's restaurants and shops crowd the narrow alleys as struggling masses of fish are poured from one container to another, and water floods onto the floor and into the shoes of the unwary. A good time to visit is early in the morning, before 9am. It's best to leave any big bags behind, since the lanes between the produce are very narrow. When you've seen enough, duck into one of the sushi bars (▷ 81–82) nearby for a Japanese breakfast.

THE BASICS

www.tsukiji-market.or.jp/tukiji_e.htm
K7
Tsukiji, Chuo-ku
Mon–Sat 5am–3pm, closed Sun, national holidays and market holidays (check at tourist offices)
Superb sushi bars and many noodle stalls
Tsukiji
Free

HIGHLIGHTS

- Fish market,
- Buyers checking fish
- Auctioneers and their entourage
- Sunrise over Sumida River
- The wholesale market
- Honganji Temple
- Pretty Namiyoke ("Wave Calm") Shrine
- Sushi breakfast

TIP

- The floors can be very wet, so wear appropriate footwear.

More to See

BRIDGESTONE MUSEUM OF ART

The founder of the Bridgestone Tire Company used some of his wealth to buy art and opened this museum in the company's building in 1952. It specializes in the French Impressionists, Post-Impressionists and Meiji-period Japanese artists who painted in Western style. A sculpture collection includes ancient Egyptian, Greek and Roman, as well as 20th-century works.

K5 1-10-1 Kyobashi, Chuo-ku (entrance on Yaesu-dori) 3563–0241 Tue–Sat 10–8, Sun and national holidays 10–6 Café nearby Kyobashi, Nihonbashi Moderate

HOUSE OF SHISEIDO

www.shiseido.co.jp/e/house-of-shiseido

On the ground floor, in an innovative, elegant space, are exhibitions that illustrate the Shiseido cosmetics company. Upstairs, you can view Shiseido's collection of nearly 2,000 artworks on a large computer screen and take a look at art and books displayed alongside products and merchandise.

J6 7-5-5 Ginza, Chuo-ku 3571–0401 Tue–Sun 11–6 Shimbashi Free

SUMIYOSHI SHRINE

Fishermen were brought to this island in the Sumida River from Osaka by Ieyasu Tokugawa to set up a fishing industry. It was they who built this shrine to the god who protects them when they are at sea.

L6 1-1-14 Tsukuda, Chuo-ku 3531–3500 Daily dawn–dusk Tsukishima Free

ZOJOJI TEMPLE

Among the city's touching sights are the rows of little statues of Mizuko Jizo, the protector of the souls of stillborn children. Some hold whirling toy windmills; others have been lovingly dressed in a special item of child's clothing.

H8 Shiba Koen, Minato-ku (lies across the street below Tokyo Tower) Daily dawn–dusk Onarimon Free

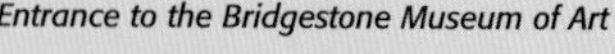

Entrance to the Bridgestone Museum of Art

Statue of Mizuko Jizo at Zojoji temple

Tsukiji/Ginza

Make an early start and walk from Tokyo's colorful fish markets down the wide Harumi-dori to Yurakucho in the heart of Ginza.

DISTANCE: 1.5 miles (2km) **ALLOW:** 4 hours

START

TSUKIJI MARKET
K7 Tsukiji-Shijo station

❶ From Tsukiji-Shijo station it is a five-minute walk to the Tsukiji market (▷ 75) where marine produce from all around the world is sold. Arrive around 7am to see the end of the tuna auctions.

❷ After a sushi breakfast, head toward Harumi-dori and turn left for the 815-yard (750m) walk to the Kabuki-za Theater building (▷ 72). See a performance if you have time.

❸ A 325-yard (300m) walk takes you to the Ginza 4-chome intersection, where you'll see two top department stores, Mitsukoshi and Wako.

❹ Another 325 yards (300m) farther on is the Sony Building (▷ 73) where you can road test your favorite computer, video game or digital camera.

❺ A final 325-yard (300m) walk brings you to Yurakucho.

❻ The Convention and Art Center at Yurakucho includes the innovative Tokyo International Forum, and if you pause a while here, chances are you'll catch some interesting event.

❼ If you're still up for more walking, take some time to explore Hibiya Park (▷ 56), just nearby from Ginza. Or, you might explore the backstreets where shopping can be fun and goods are often less expensive than at the department stores.

❽ Wander back to Ginza station at your leisure and look out for a budget *tachi-gui* eatery where you can stand and dine with the locals.

END

YURAKUCHO MARION
J6 Ginza

Shopping

GINZA-YURAKUCHO
For the famous department stores on Chuo-dori and in Yurakucho, and specialist shops, craft shops and antiques shops, from Ginza 4-chome through 7-chome.
J6 Ginza, Higashi-Ginza Yurakucho

INTERNATIONAL ARCADE
Thirty shops selling crafts and souvenirs, from the superb to the average. Several pearl shops.
J6 1-7-23 Uchisaiwaicho, Chiyoda-ku Daily 11–9 Hibiya

ITO-YA
One to visit for stationery, wrapping paper and greeting cards—Japanese and imported. Art supplies and some ingenious desk accessories.
J6 2-7-15 Ginza, Chuo-ku 3561–8311 Mon–Sat 9.30–7, Sun 10–6 Ginza

KORANSHA
Fine ceramics, especially flower and bird patterns from Arita in Kyushu.
K6 5-12-12 Ginza, Chuo-ku 3543–0951 Mon–Sat 9.30–6.30 Higashi-Ginza

KYUKYODO
Beautiful handmade papers and everything needed for calligraphy.
J6 5-7-4 Ginza, Chuo-ku 3571–4429 Daily 10–6 Ginza

MARUZEN
Imported books, travel books and others about every aspect of Japanese life. Good for wood-block prints.
K5 2-1-10 Nihonbashi, Chuo-ku 3272–3316 Daily 10–7 Nihonbashi

MATSUYA
Colorful department store favored by younger customers. The basement food hall sells excellent boxed meals at sensible prices.
J6 3-6-1 Ginza, Chuo-ku 3567–1211 Mon–Wed, Fri 10–6, Sat–Sun and national holidays 10–6.30 Ginza

MIKIMOTO
This is the big name in the field of cultured pearls, with top prices.
J6 4-5-5 Ginza, Chuo-ku 3535–4611 Thu–Tue 10–6 Ginza

EVERYDAY QUALITY

If the price of fine porcelain and lacquerware comes as a shock, look instead at the everyday versions sold in street markets and department stores. The Japanese sense of color and form extends to these, too, and quality is usually faultless. Even the disposable baskets and boxes used for take-away meals can be minor craftworks. Special hand-made and decorative papers, in the form of wrappings, stationery, boxes, dolls, fans and origami designs make good gifts—light, unbreakable and reasonably priced.

MITSUKOSHI
Department store founded in the 17th century, with selections of toys, stationery, kimonos, sportswear and a fine food hall. It even has its own subway station.
K4 1-4-1 Nihonbashi-Muromachi, Chuo-ku 3241–3311 Tue–Sat 10–6, Sun and holidays 10–6.30 Mitsukoshi-mae

SHIODOME
Toyko's futuristic, urban shopping, entertainment and dining precinct includes dozens of brand-name shops, great restaurants and the Nihon TV headquarters. Nearby is Tokyo Tower (▷ 74), Zojoji Temple (▷ 76) and piers that are departure points for Tokyo Bay cruises.
J7 Shimbashi

TAKASHIMAYA
The basement food hall of this department store has Fauchon and Fortnum & Mason counters. Elegant displays and opulent surroundings, immaculately turned-out staff and boutiques with famous-name fashions.
K5 2-4-1 Nihonbashi, Chuo-ku 3211–4111 Thu–Tue 10–7 Nihonbashi

Entertainment and Nightlife

GINZA
The prices in the clubs and top restaurants are legendary, and prohibitive for anyone not on an unlimited expense account. Others can enjoy the street scene, find a fast-food or budget restaurant and enjoy a drink in one of the affordable bars or big beer halls.

300 BAR
Over 100 kinds of food and drinks, all priced at ¥300, at this standing bar. There is no entrance fee and no time limit.
J6 B1 Fazenda Building, 5-9-11 Ginza, Chuo-ku 3572-6300 Mon–Sat 5pm–2am, Sun and national holidays 5–11pm Ginza

APPLE STORE GINZA
As well as offering free wireless internet on the top floor, this multilevel showroom is packed with the latest gizmos to try and/or buy. Spend a fun hour or two here.
J6 3-5-12 Ginza, Chuo-ku 5159-8200 Daily 10–9 Ginza

CLUB MAIKO
One of the few "geisha" bars that welcomes foreigners. A package deal, which includes entrance, snacks and drinks, costs ¥8,000.
J6 Plaza Bldg. 4F, 7-7-6 Ginza, Chuo-ku 3574-7745 Mon–Thu 4.30pm–12.30am, Fri 4.30pm–2am Ginza

GINZA SAPPORO LION
Ignore the German decor and check out the locals who come to unwind here after work. Snacks include *yakitori* (grilled chicken on skewers), sausage and spaghetti.
J6 7-9-20 Ginza 3571-2590 Mon–Sat 11.30–11, Sun 11.30–10.30 Ginza

HAKUHINKAN THEATER
This popular little theater specializes in musicals as well as choral and popular concerts. The bar offers drinks and light snacks before the show. Try to book in advance.

TICKET AGENCIES

For most theaters, concert halls and major sports arenas, you can reserve tickets up to the day before the performance at agencies such as:

Play Guide Honten
K6 2-6-4 Ginza, Chuo-ku 3561-8821 Ginza

Ticket Park Hakuhinkan
J6 8-8-11 Ginza, Chuo-ku 3571-1003 Shimbashi

On the day of the performance, telephone the venue and arrange to collect the tickets there; if you have a problem making yourself understood, ask someone at your hotel to make the call.

J6 8-8-11 Ginza, Chuo-ku 3571-8008 Daily 6–10.30pm Shimbashi

IRISH TIMES
An Irish-theme pub with good craic and live music that attracts the after-work crowd.
J6 2-9-16 Shimbashi, Minato-ku 3500-0200 Mon–Thu 4.30pm–12.30am, Fri 4.30pm–2am Shimbashi

JICOO
This bar is actually a boat that goes back and forth across Tokyo Bay, leaving Hinode Pier, a short walk from Hinode station on the Yurikamome light rail line, each hour. A boarding fee of ¥2,500 includes one drink.
J8 Hinode Pier 0120-049-490 Thu–Sat 8–11pm Hinode (light rail)

KIRIN CITY
Popular with locals for after-work drinks. Great selection of beers and basic foods.
J6 Bunshodo Building 2F, 3-4-12 Ginza, Chuo-ku 3562-2593 Mon–Sat 6pm–midnight Ginza

TWENTY EIGHT
One of the most stylish hotel bars in Tokyo, part of the Conrad Hotel, with good music and *Lost in Translation* views.
J7 1-9-1 Higashi-Shimbashi, Minato-ku 6388-8000 Shimbashi

Restaurants

PRICES

Prices are approximate, based on a 3-course meal for one person.

¥¥¥	over ¥8,000
¥¥	¥3,000–¥8,000
¥	under ¥3,000

CHIANG MAI (¥¥)

Customers are crammed into two small rooms to savor the standard dishes, cooked by two Thai chefs. Try the *tom yam gung* shrimp soup and the spicy chicken.
J6 1-6-10 Yurakucho, Chiyoda-ku 3580–0456 Daily 11.30–11 Hibiya

DAIDAIYA (¥¥)

Cool avant-garde interiors and an à la carte menu that includes sushi and tempura, handmade noodles and grilled meats.
J7 2F Ginza Nine No. 1 Bldg, 8-5-Saki, Ginza, Chuo-ku 5537–3566 Open Mon–Sat 5pm–1am (last orders midnight), Sun 5pm–midnight Shimbashi

EDOGIN (¥¥)

Its proximity to the fish market means fresh ingredients and this busy no-frills eatery, packed with locals, has an illustrated menu of set meals. Be sure to try some of the extensive range of sushi, and the *nigiri-zushi teishoku* (mixed sushi platter), which comes with soup and pickled vegetables.
K6 4-5-12 Tsukiji, Chuo-ku 3543–4401 Daily 11–9.30 Tsukiji

GANKO (¥¥)

The sushi and sashimi ingredients used in this restaurant come from all over Japan and are always fresh. You can order in English.
J6 4-4-1 Ginza, Chuo-ku 3564–5678 Daily 11–10.30 Yurakucho

IRIMOYA (¥¥)

Set in a traditional old building, dishes here are based on organic fish and chicken and fresh vegetables. A variety of sake and *shochu* is available.
J6 3F Ginza Lion Building, 7-9-20 Ginza, Chuo-ku 3571–4384 Mon–Fri 5–11pm, Sat 3–11pm, Sun 3–10pm Ginza

ETIQUETTE 1

- After wiping your fingers on the moist towel (*oshibori*) brought before your meal, roll it up and keep it for use as a napkin.
- Drink soup from the bowl as if it were a cup. Pick out solid pieces with chopsticks.
- Slurping soup and noodles is considered acceptable and normal.
- To eat rice, hold the bowl close to your mouth and use chopsticks.
- Don't point with chopsticks, or lick the ends, or put the ends that go in your mouth into a communal dish.

KYUBEI (¥¥¥)

Founded many years ago, and still going strong, Kyubei specializes in some of the most expertly made sushi around.
K6 8-7-6 Ginza, Chuo-ku 3571–6523 Mon–Sat 11.30–2, 5–10 Higashi-Ginza

LINTARO (¥¥)

Lintaro Mizuhama is the friendly owner of the restaurant, and he is often to be found chatting with diners or directing the service. The food is Italian but with Japanese notes in its presentation and flavors. The superbly fresh salads and vegetables are from the restaurant's special gardens.
J6 5-9-15 Ginza, Chuo-ku 3571–2037 Daily 11.30–10; closed New Year holiday Ginza

MONSOON (¥¥)

The English-language menu features Southeast Asian and Japanese cuisine, including satay, lemon-grass shrimp, curries and a selection of vegetarian dishes.
J6 1-2-3 Ginza, Chuo-ku 5524–3631 Daily 11.30am–5pm Ginza

MUNAKATA (¥¥)

Try the cheaper lunchtime meals at this intimate and popular *kaiseki* (haute cuisine) restaurant.

They do good boxed lunches here.
J6 Mitsui Urban Hotel basement, 8-6-15 Ginza, Chou-ku 3574–9356 Daily 11.30–4, 5–10 Shimbashi or Hibiya

THE SIAM (¥)
This one has been around for years and is still going strong, serving tasty Thai food at prices that are economical—for Ginza—especially at lunchtime.
K6 World Town Building 8F, 5-8-17 Ginza, Chuo-ku 3572–4101 Daily 11.30–2, 5.30–9.30 Higashi-Ginza

SUSHI DAI (¥)
Try the *setto*, a set sushi course with tuna, eel, shrimps and other morsels, plus rolls of tuna and rice in seaweed.
K6 Tsukiji Fish Market No 6, Tsukiji 3547–6797 Mon–Sat 5am–2pm Tsukiji

TAKARA (¥¥)
Located on one of the lower floors of the stylish Tokyo International Forum, Takara is well known for its sake but also offers tapas dishes and a selection of *izakaya* treats (snacks).
J5/J6 Tokyo International Forum B1 Concourse, 3-5-1 Marunouchi, Chiyoda-ku 5223–9888 Mon–Fri 11.30–2.30, 5–11, Sat–Sun and national holidays 11.30–3, 5–10 Tokyo or Yurakucho

TAKENO (¥)
Located near the central fish market, this restaurant serves good-size helpings of sushi, *sashimi* and tempura. A good place to go after a look around the market.
K6 6-21-2 Tsukiji, Chuo-ku 3541–8698 Mon–Sat 11–9; closed market and national holidays Tsukiji

TARAFUKU (¥¥¥)
Fugu (blowfish) is the specialty of this traditional restaurant, although seasonal specials substitute during summer months when it is not available.
J6 7-8-18 Ginza 3573–0129 Mon–Fri 11.30–2, 4.30–11; Sat–Sun 4–10 Ginza

TEN ICHI (¥¥¥)
This is Tokyo's most renowned restaurant for tempura—battered-and-fried pieces of seafood and vegetables.
J6 6-6-5 Ginza, Chuo-ku 3571–1949 Daily 11.30–9.30 Ginza

ETIQUETTE 2

• Don't leave chopsticks crossed or standing upright in a bowl.

• If you can't manage something with chopsticks, ask for a knife (*naifu*), fork (*foku*) or spoon (*supun*).

• Never blow your nose in a restaurant. Find somewhere to hide first.

• Pour drinks for your companions; leave it to them to pour yours. When they do, it's polite to hold your glass up to be filled.

T.G.I. FRIDAY'S (¥)
This US chain serves all the authentic American cuisine you'd expect, along with original cocktails and beers and spirits.
J6 1-2F Tabulu-Kan, 8-9-4 Ginza, Chuo-ku 5537–5955 Sun–Thu 11.30am–midnight, Fri 11.30am–3am, Sat 11.30am–1am Ginza

WASAI GINZA (¥¥)
Luxurious Japanese decor and a health-conscious menu, which includes dishes based on fresh vegetables. The drinks menu features a selection of Japanese sake.
J6 B1 Kawabata-Shinkan Bldg, 8-5-21 Ginza, Chuo-ku 6253–8570 Mon–Fri 5pm–4am, Sat 5–11.30; closed Sun and national holidays Ginza or Shimbashi

YOSHINARI (¥¥)
A *kushiyaki* restaurant specializing in grilled meat, fish and vegetables served on skewers, and *nabe*, a souplike hot-pot dish. Serves sake and other Japanese-style spirits.
J6 B1 Tousei Building, 8-10-7 Ginza, Chuo-ku 5537–1566 Mon–Fri 6–11pm; Sat 6–10pm, closed Sun and national holidays Shimbashi

Suburban Ueno, away from the fashionable shopping and entertainment districts, throws light on the ordinary citizens of Tokyo and is home to Ueno Park with its cultural institutions.

Sights	86–93
Walk	94
Shopping	95
Entertainment and Nightlife	95
Restaurants	96

Top 25 TOP 25

Asakusa Kannon Temple ▷ **86**

Edo-Tokyo Museum ▷ **88**

National Museum of Western Art ▷ **89**

Tokyo National Museum ▷ **90**

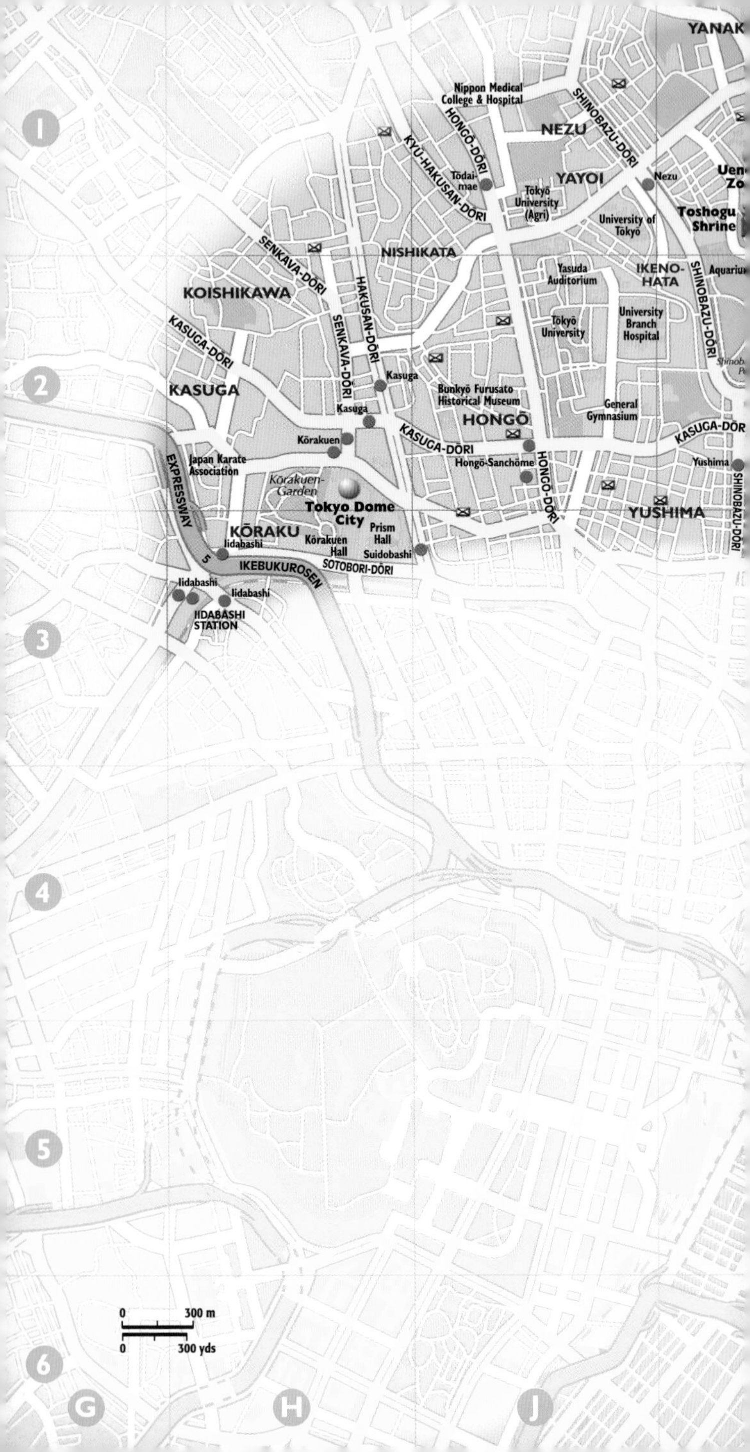

YANAK
Nippon Medical College & Hospital
SHINOBAZU-DŌRI
NEZU
HONGŌ-DŌRI
KYŪ-HAKUSAN-DŌRI
Tōdai-mae
YAYOI
Nezu
Tōkyō University (Agri)
University of Tōkyō
Toshogu Shrine
SENKAVA-DŌRI
NISHIKATA
KOISHIKAWA
HAKUSAN-DŌRI
Yasuda Auditorium
IKENO-HATA
Aquariu
KASUGA-DŌRI
SENKAVA-DŌRI
Tōkyō University
University Branch Hospital
Kasuga
Bunkyō Furusato Historical Museum
KASUGA
Kasuga
HONGŌ
General Gymnasium
Kōrakuen
KASUGA-DŌRI
KASUGA-DŌR
Japan Karate Association
Hongō-Sanchōme
Yushima
EXPRESSWAY
Kōrakuen-Garden
Tokyo Dome City
HONGŌ-DŌRI
YUSHIMA
SHINOBAZU-DŌRI
KŌRAKU
Iidabashi
Kōrakuen Hall
Prism Hall
Suidobashi
5
IKEBUKUROSEN
SOTOBORI-DŌRI
Iidabashi
Iidabashi
IIDABASHI STATION
1
2
3
4
5
6
0
300 m
0
300 yds
G
H
J

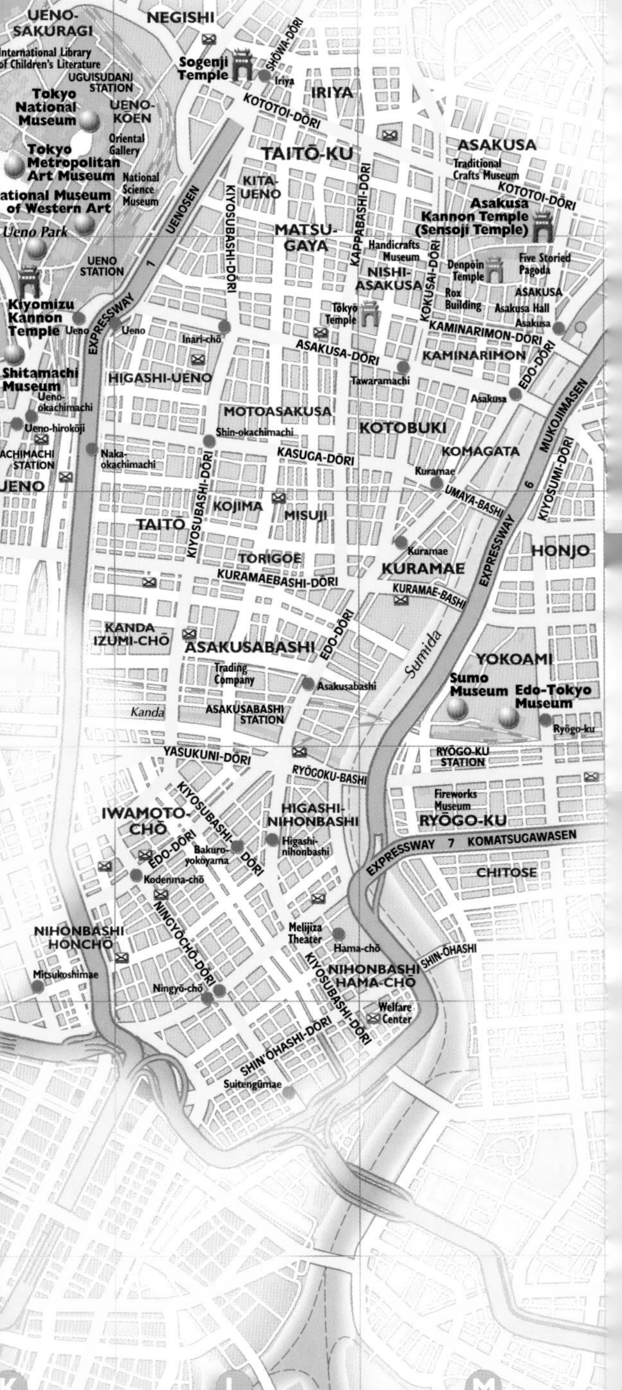
UENO-SAKURAGI
NEGISHI
International Library of Children's Literature
UGUISUDANI STATION
Sogenji Temple
SHŌWA-DŌRI
Iriya
IRIYA
Tokyo National Museum
UENO-KŌEN
KOTOTOI-DŌRI
Oriental Gallery
Tokyo Metropolitan Art Museum
TAITŌ-KU
ASAKUSA
Traditional Crafts Museum
National Science Museum
KITA-UENO
KOTOTOI-DŌRI
National Museum of Western Art
UENOSEN
KIYOSUBASHI-DŌRI
KAPPABASHI-DŌRI
Asakusa Kannon Temple (Sensoji Temple)
Ueno Park
MATSU-GAYA
Handicrafts Museum
KOKUSAI-DŌRI
UENO STATION
NISHI-ASAKUSA
Denpoin Temple
Five Storied Pagoda
Rox Building
ASAKUSA
Asakusa Hall
Kiyomizu Kannon Temple
Ueno
Ueno
Tokyo Temple
Asakusa
EXPRESSWAY 1
Inari-chō
KAMINARIMON-DŌRI
ASAKUSA-DŌRI
KAMINARIMON
EDO-DŌRI
Shitamachi Museum
HIGASHI-UENO
Tawaramachi
MUKOJIMASEN
Asakusa
Ueno-okachimachi
MOTOASAKUSA
Ueno-hirokōji
Shin-okachimachi
KOTOBUKI
KACHIMACHI STATION
Naka-okachimachi
KASUGA-DŌRI
KOMAGATA
KIYOSUMI-DŌRI
UENO
Kuramae
UMAYA-BASHI
EXPRESSWAY 6
KOJIMA
MISUJI
TAITŌ
KIYOSUBASHI-DŌRI
Kuramae
HONJO
TORIGOE
KURAMAEBASHI-DŌRI
KURAMAE
KURAMAE-BASHI
KANDA IZUMI-CHŌ
EDO-DŌRI
ASAKUSABASHI
Sumida
YOKOAMI
Trading Company
Asakusabashi
Sumo Museum
Edo-Tokyo Museum
Kanda
ASAKUSABASHI STATION
Ryōgo-ku
YASUKUNI-DŌRI
RYŌGO-KU STATION
RYŌGOKU-BASHI
Fireworks Museum
IWAMOTO-CHŌ
KIYOSUBASHI-DŌRI
HIGASHI-NIHONBASHI
RYŌGO-KU
EDO-DŌRI
Bakuro-yokoyama
Higashi-nihonbashi
EXPRESSWAY 7 KOMATSUGAWASEN
Kodenma-chō
CHITOSE
NINGYŌCHŌ-DŌRI
NIHONBASHI HONCHŌ
Melijiza Theater
Hama-chō
SHIN-ŌHASHI
KIYOSUBASHI-DŌRI
NIHONBASHI HAMA-CHŌ
Mitsukoshimae
Ningyō-chō
Welfare Center
SHIN'ŌHASHI-DŌRI
Suitengūmae
K
L
M

Asakusa Kannon Temple

HIGHLIGHTS

- Nakamise-dori: stalls
- Hozomon (gate)
- Five-story pagoda
- Worshippers "washing" in smoke
- Main Sensoji shrine
- Tokinokane Bell
- Denbo-in Temple Garden
- Chingodo Shrine
- Rice-cracker makers
- Clowns and acrobats

TIP

- This is a great place to shop for Japanese souvenirs; bring some spending money.

Old Japan lives on in the bustling Asakusa quarter. The temple ceremonies are more colorful than those elsewhere in Tokyo, and there's always a crowd here intent on shopping at the many stalls.

The people's favorite Now dedicated to uniting the competing Buddhist factions, the Asakusa Kannon Temple (Sensoji Temple) has its origins in the 7th century. Pilgrims came from all over Japan, and the Asakusa neighborhood set about entertaining them—providing food and lodging, theaters, houses of pleasure and *onsen* (baths). The area, leveled by earthquakes, bombs and fires, was always rebuilt to resemble the original and remains a favorite haunt of out-of-town visitors and the foreigners who discover it. Late afternoon is a good time to come, when dozens of food

The five-story pagoda rises above colorful flower beds (far left); the Main Hall of Asakusa Kannon Temple (top middle); traveling by rickshaw (top right); fans for sale on Nakamise-dori (below middle); visitors crowd around the temple's Bronze Urn (below right)

stands send out tantalizing aromas and circus performers amuse the crowds.

The sights Near the subway station, opposite the entrance to the temple grounds, is the local information center. Across the road and through the Kaminarimon gate is Nakamise-dori, a pedestrian street lined with about 150 fascinating stalls selling traditional Japanese clothing, snacks, papercraft, fans and dolls, which leads to a second gate, Hozomon, with an elegant five-story pagoda. Straight ahead lies the main shrine hall, just beyond a great bronze incense burner wreathed in smoke, which visitors wave over themselves in the belief that it has curative properties. To the right (west) of the temple is Asakusa-jinja, a Shinto shrine. The east gate, Nitenmon, survives largely intact from the year 1618.

THE BASICS

M1
2-3-1 Asakusa, Taito-ku
3842–0181
Daily 6am–dusk
The area is noted for good restaurants
Asakusa
Good
Free
Included in many city tours

Edo-Tokyo Museum

A swish glass-covered escalator at the museum entrance (left); exterior view (right)

THE BASICS

www.edo-tokyo-museum.or.jp/english
M3
1-4-1 Yokoami, Sumida-ku
3626–9974
Daily 9.30–5.30 (Sat until 7.30); closed Mon and Dec 28–Jan 4
Restaurant and café
Ryogoku
Excellent
Inexpensive
Volunteer guide service for the permanent exhibit

HIGHLIGHTS

- Audiovisual hall
- Middle-Jomon period dwelling
- Nihombashi Bridge
- Earthquake display
- Reconstructed Tokyo
- Edo Castle

TIP

- Free services include lockers, baby carriages, audio-guides and wheelchairs.

This state-of-the-art museum, opened in 1993, celebrates the history and culture of Tokyo in such a dramatic and interesting way that it certainly merits the reputation as the city's premier history museum.

The building The futuristic museum was inspired by an old warehouse and rises up to 203ft (62m), about the same height as Edo Castle's topmost tower. The museum covers Tokyo's history from the 17th century to the present.

Earthquakes and aesthetics You enter the permanent exhibition space, spread over two floors, via a reproduction of a wooden Nihombashi bridge, a structure made famous by countless woodblock prints. The area beyond is divided into three sections—History Zone, Edo Zone, and Tokyo Zone—each filled with diverse displays ranging from business life, the aesthetics of Edo, and urban culture and pleasure. Displays covering civilization and enlightenment are not far from those covering the two great 20th-century disasters to befall the city, the 1923 Kanto earthquake and the firebombing of Tokyo in 1945. Original material and images are included, as well as large-scale models and faithful reproductions. Special interest exhibitions and lectures are regularly held, and in the audiovisual hall there are three-dimensional images of the past. A library on Level 7, with more than 140,000 books and magazines plus microfilm covering the history of Edo-Tokyo, is open to the public.

Rodin's The Thinker *is in the collection (left); the modernist design of the museum (right)*

National Museum of Western Art

You may not have come to Tokyo to see masterpieces of European art, but the collection of this museum, mainly formed by one visionary in the early 20th century, is far too good to miss.

The museum The National Museum of Western Art (Kokuritsu Seiyo Bijutsukan) is on the right of the main gate to Ueno Park from the JR station. The modernist concrete building, designed by Le Corbusier, holds the art collection of Kojiro Matsukata. Matsukata was a successful businessman who spent a lot of time in Europe in the early 20th century and developed a passion for the work of the French Impressionists. His collection eventually included some of the finest paintings by Monet, Renoir, Gauguin (in his pre-Tahiti period) and Van Gogh, more than 50 of the most famous Rodin bronzes (including *The Thinker* and *The Burghers of Calais*) and El Greco's *The Crucifixion*. Matsukata kept them in Europe, but after World War II they were brought to Japan and bequeathed to the nation in his will. The museum was opened in 1959.

The growing collection Kojiro Matsukata's acquisitions are still the museum's greatest strength, but subsequent major purchases have filled the gaps in the collection. There are works by Old Masters, including Tintoretto, Rubens and El Greco; moderns are represented by Max Ernst, Jackson Pollock and others. You can stroll among the sculptures in the courtyard; inside, good lighting does justice to the wonderful works of art.

THE BASICS

www.nmwa.go.jp
K1
7-7 Ueno-koen, Taito-ku
3828–5131
Tue–Sun 9.30–5 (Fri until 8pm); closed Tue if Mon a national holiday, and Dec 28–Jan 1
Drinks stand; snacks outside
Ueno
Ueno (Park exit)
Good
Moderate

HIGHLIGHTS

- *Crucifixion*, El Greco
- *The Loving Cup*, D. G. Rossetti
- Rodin bronzes
- *Landscape of Brittany*, Gauguin
- *On the Boat*, Monet
- *The Port of St Tropez*, Signac

TIP

- Be sure to visit the Museum Shop and the Café Suiren.

Tokyo National Museum

TOP 25

HIGHLIGHTS

- Jomon-era clay masks
- Terra-cotta burial figures
- Decorative tiles
- Imari ware
- Noh costumes, 16th–18th centuries
- Sword collection
- Han Dynasty stone reliefs
- Tang Dynasty horses and camel

TIP

- Allow yourself sufficient time to see this large collection properly.

A great museum sparks your interest in fields you never thought about before. Here you can learn about every aspect of Japanese art and archaeology and view a fine collection of other Asian art. Simply breathtaking.

The Japanese collection The central Honkan building displays the finest of Japanese art: Not only painting and sculpture, but calligraphy, ceramics including the celebrated Imari ware, kimonos, swords, armor and *ukiyo-e* (woodblock prints). There are exquisite noh theater costumes, some dating from the 16th century.

Archaeology The Heiseikan, the newest of the five main buildings of the Tokyo National Museum (Tokyo Kokuritsu Hakubutsukan), was built in

An ornate suit of early Japanese armor (far left); the attractive setting of the Tokyo National Museum (top middle); an early figurine on display in the museum (top right); Cherry Blossom Viewing at Goten Yama Hill *by Toyohiro Utagawa (bottom left); a 17th-century Imari ware dish (bottom middle); an architectural detail (bottom right)*

1999 and forms a new wing to the left of the Honkan building. It houses relics found all over Japan: Prehistoric flint axes, pottery from around 3,000BC, bronze bells and sword blades. Many terra-cotta burial figures—musicians, horses and wild boars—date from the 3rd to 6th centuries.

Other Asian art The Toyokan building includes exhibits of Chinese jade and bronzes, 1st-century stone reliefs, Tang Dynasty ceramic horses and a camel, precious porcelain and textiles. Korea, Southeast Asia, Iran, Iraq and even ancient Egypt are represented. Gondara Buddhist sculpture from Central Asia shows the influence of ancient Greek art during and after the time of Alexander the Great. Be sure to look inside the Hyokeikan building, opened in 1909 as a memorial for the marriage of the Meiji Crown Prince in 1900.

THE BASICS

www.tnm.jp
K1
13–9 Ueno Koen, Taito-ku
3822–1111
Tue–Sun 9.30–5; closed Tue if Mon a national holiday, and Dec 28–Jan 1
A small restaurant serves snacks and light meals
Ueno
Ueno
Good
Moderate

More to See

KIYOMIZU KANNON TEMPLE
Bullet holes in the Kuromon gate date from the 1868 battle for the hill. Childless women pray to a Kannon figure in the temple, and, if they subsequently have a baby, return to leave a doll in gratitude. Every September 25 the accumulated dolls are burned in a great bonfire.
K2 Ueno Koen, Taito-ku Daily dawn–dusk Plenty nearby Ueno Free

SHITAMACHI MUSEUM
A compact museum recording working-class life of a century ago. Check out the merchant's shop, sweet shop and coppersmith's home. You can handle everyday objects.
K2 2-1 Ueno Koen, Taito-ku 3823–7451 Tue–Sun 9.30–4.30 Snack bar Ueno Inexpensive

SOGENJI TEMPLE
This is also known as Kappa Temple, a name derived from the legendary water sprites who helped to drain the once extensive marshes that once covered this area.
L1 3-7-2 Matsugaya, Taito-ku 3841–2035 Daily dawn–dusk Tawaramachi Free

SUMO MUSEUM
A store of records, relics and pictures of past *yokozuna*—the grand masters of sumo wrestling—is housed in the building, which is also the main venue for matches. You may see some of today's big men arriving in their stretch limousines.
M3 1-3-28 Yokoami, Sumida-ku 3622–0366 Mon–Fri 10–4.30; closed during tournaments, except to ticket holders Snacks Ryogoku Free

TOKYO DOME CITY
This attraction has a giant roller-coaster, the Ultra Twister and loop-the-loop train, as well as gentler rides for younger children. The entry ticket does not include the cost of rides.
H2 1-3-61 Korakuen, Bunkyo-ku 3817–6001 Daily 10–9 Snack bars and food stands Korakuen, Suidobashi Suidobashi Expensive

Tombstones at Sogenji Temple

Gate near the entrance to the National Sumo Museum

UENO ★ MORE TO SEE

TOKYO METROPOLITAN ART MUSEUM

The spacious galleries here accommodate touring exhibitions and modern art shows. There is also a small permanent collection of 20th-century Japanese art, mostly in Western styles.

K1 Ueno Koen, Taito-ku 3823–6921 Tue–Sun 9–5 Café Ueno Free (except special exhibitions)

TOSHOGU SHRINE

This shrine, dating from 1651, is dedicated to the first Tokugawa shogun, Ieyasu, who died in 1616 and was quickly proclaimed divine. One of few vestiges of the early Edo period, it somehow escaped destruction in the 1868 battle between adherents of the emperor and those of the Tokugawas, when most buildings on Ueno hill were burned down. The path from the *torii* is lined by more than 200 stone and bronze lanterns.

K1 9-88 Ueno Koen, Taito-ku 3822–3455 Daily 9.30–4.30 Food stands nearby Ueno Moderate

UENO PARK

The park, which opened to the public in 1873, is the home of several museums, concert halls and a zoo (▷ below). In spring, locals come by the thousands to admire the cherry blossoms. Check out the ducks and geese on Shinobazu Pond, where species from the Arctic and Siberia spend the winter.

K1 Ueno Koen, Taito-ku Daily 5am–11pm Restaurants and food stands Ueno Ueno (Park exit more convenient than subway) Free (museums, shrines and the zoo charge entry fees)

UENO ZOO

Japan's first zoo, which opened in the late 19th century, displays more than 350 species including the popular giant pandas, which are fed daily at 3.30; they're not on view on Friday. There is an open-air area where children can stroke the animals.

K1 Ueno Koen 3828–5171 Tue–Sun 9.30–5 Café Ueno Moderate

Linear Gale and Thunder Dolphin roller-coaster rides in the Fun Park at Tokyo Dome City

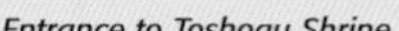

Entrance to Toshogu Shrine

A Stroll around Ueno

Sample local shopping at Ameyoko, stroll through beautiful Ueno Park, visit shrines and spend time exploring Tokyo's finest museum.

DISTANCE: 1.9 miles (2.5km) **ALLOW:** 6 hours

START

YUSHIMA STATION

K2 Yushima station

❶ From Yushima station, head straight for the Yushima Tenmangu Shrine, which is dedicated to the God of Learning.

❷ Now take a 12-minute walk to the Ameyoko Market (▷ 95), where you can browse household goods and fresh produce and see where the locals do their shopping.

❸ After a snack, head south for the excellent Shitamachi Museum (▷ 92), a small folk museum displaying old household goods and toys.

❹ Walk northward 545 yards (500m) around the edge of the pond towards Toshogu Shrine (▷ 93), with more than 200 stone and bronze lanterns.

❺ Walk another 545 yards (500m) to the Tokyo National Museum (▷ 90).

❻ Take time at the museum to fully appreciate some of the nation's treasures housed here. You might be ready for a lunch stop at the museum restaurant.

❼ The walk to Ueno station is around 12 minutes from the museum, but you might wish to make a short detour to see nearby Ueno Zoo (▷ 93).

❽ Or, you might explore the backstreets of Ueno where goods are often less expensive than in the department stores.

END

UENO STATION

K2 Ueno station

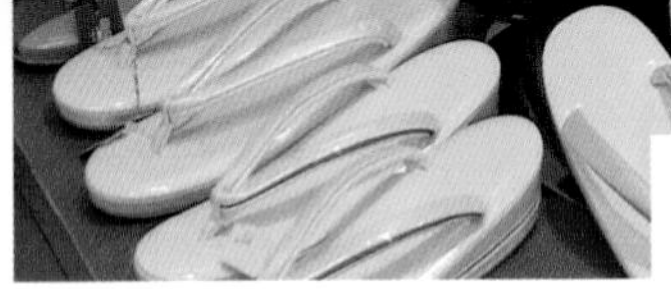

Shopping

AMEYOKO MARKET

The Ameyoko market runs under the elevated JR Yamanote tracks, from Ueno station to Okachimachi station. It is packed with stalls selling food, household goods, clothes, footwear, jewelry, watches, cameras and electronic equipment–almost anything, in fact. Bargaining is not unexpected and vendor competition is spirited and friendly.

K2 Ueno

KAPPABASHI

What the Tsukiji Fish Market (▷ 75) is to fish, Kappabashi is to plates, pans, chopsticks, knives, lanterns, signs and everything the restaurant business needs except food–the shops here sell only the plastic variety. A huge head crowned with a chef's hat stands on top of a tall building to mark the beginning of Kappabashi-dori.

M2 Kappabashi-dori, Taito-ku Tawaramachi

NAKAMISE-DORI

Nakamise-dori, located between the red lantern at the Thunder Gate and the main hall of the Sensoji Temple, is a pedestrian street of stalls offering a wide range of traditional souvenirs. The temple grounds are always full of people shopping, buying fortunes and praying. Take a walk around the fascinating back streets for a glimpse of old Japan.

M2 Asakusa

Entertainment and Nightlife

ASAKUSA KANNON ONSEN

A large and very hot bath, esteemed for its curative properties.

M2 2-7-26 Asakusa, Taito-ku 3844–4141 Daily 6.30–6.30 Asakusa

FLAMME D'OR ASAHI

Traditional beer hall where locals relax.

M2 Asahi Brewery, 1 Azumabashi, Sumida-ku Daily 11.30–11.30 Asakusa

KOKUGIKAN SUMO HALL

Six tournaments annually, each lasting 15 days, are held here in January, May and September.

M3 1-3-28 Yokoami, Sumida-ku 3623–5111 10–6 (main bouts 3–6) Ryogoku

SUMO

Literally "fat power," this form of wrestling was originally practiced at Shinto shrines and is surrounded by time-honored ceremony. After purification and other rituals, the two huge contenders collide, each intent on unbalancing the other and tipping him over or forcing him from the ring. *Tokyo Basho* tournaments take place in January, May and September. Tickets for better seats are expensive, but they include a box meal.

TOKYO BUNKA KAIKAN

Located at the entrance to Ueno Park. Seats 2,300 in the main hall, 700 in a smaller auditorium. The foyer shop sells sheet music and souvenirs.

L2 5-45 Ueno Koen, Taito-ku 3828–2111 Ueno

TOKYO DOME

www.tokyo-dome.co.jp/e/dome

This 55,000-seat stadium, Japan's biggest concert venue, hosts more than 60 baseball games a year as well as many international sports events and festivals.

J3 1-3-61 Koraku, Bunkyo-ku 3811–2111 Suidobashi

Restaurants

PRICES

Prices are approximate, based on a 3-course meal for one person.

¥¥¥ over ¥8,000
¥¥ ¥3,000–¥8,000
¥ under ¥3,000

FUTABA (¥)

Ueno is known especially for *tonkatsu*, fried pork cutlet, eaten with rice, soup and pickled vegetables; this is one of the oldest restaurants serving it.

K2 4-4-12 Ueno, Taito-ku 3835–2672 Daily 11.30–2.30, 5–7.30 Ueno

IZU'EI (¥¥)

This traditional Japanese restaurant offers delicious charcoal-grilled eel as well as sushi and tempura, and set meals. Choose from the display case outside, take a seat and dine with views over Shinobazu Pond.

K2 2-12-22 Ueno, across from Shitamachi Museum 3831–0954 Daily 11–9.30 Ueno

KUREMUTSU (¥¥)

The specialties in this traditional house with a delightful courtyard, are grilled fish, *sashimi* and *kaiseki* meals. Perfect for real Japanese food but reservations essential.

M2 2-2-13 Asakusa, Nakamise 3842–0906 Tue–Sun 4–9.30 Asakusa

MANTRA (¥)

From 11am to 3pm, you can enjoy a variety of dishes from the all-you-can-eat buffet. The Indian menu includes meat or vegetarian set meals, plus inexpensive curries and tandoori.

K2 4-9-6 Ueno, F3, Nagafuji Building 3835–0818 Daily 11–9.30 Ueno

NAKASEI (¥¥¥)

A famous and long-established tempura restaurant near Nakamise-dori. Follow your nose and be prepared to wait. There is often a line outside. Lunch is best—for economy and because the area shuts down early in the evening.

M2 1-39-13 Asakusa, Taito-ku 3841–4015 Wed–Mon 12–8 Asakusa

TOFU

In Japan, tofu comes in two varieties. The soft *kinugoshi* tofu, used in soup, has a silky texture. The firmer *momen* is stir-fried or used in hot pots, or eaten by itself. A local favorite is *hiyayakko*—blocks of tofu, either *kinugoshi* or *momen*, topped with grated ginger and sliced spring onion. *Abura-age* is a very thinly sliced, deep-fried tofu used in miso soup or for *inarizushi* (sushi rice in a seasoned tofu pouch).

NAMIKI YABU SOBA (¥)

A branch of the renowned Yabu Soba, this affordable eatery specializes in tempura *soba* dishes.

M2 2-11-9 Kaminarimon, Asakusa 3841–1340 Daily lunch, dinner Asakusa

OMIYA (¥¥)

This French restaurant, in traditional Asakusa, has tasty beef dishes and a great choice of interesting wines.

M2 2-1-3 Asakusa, Asakusa 3844–0038 Mon–Sat 11.30–1.30, 5.30–8.30 Asakusa

SANSADA (¥¥)

Located beside the Kurodaya paper shop, at the gate to the Asakusa Kannon Temple, this restaurant specializes in tempura. Make your selection outside, then be seated on traditional tatami upstairs, or at tables on the first floor.

M2 1-2-2 Asakusa 3841–3400 Daily 11–9 Asakusa

UENO SEIYOKEN GRILL (¥¥¥)

Classic French cuisine, an English-language menu, a good selection of French wines, views over the park, plus classical music in the background.

K2 In Ueno Park, between Toshogu Shrine and Kiyomizu Temple 3821–2181 Daily 11–8 Ueno

Farther Afield

Suburban and out-of-town attractions include the pretty Rikugien Garden to the north of the city, the futuristic shopping and entertainment precinct of Odaiba and the ever-popular Tokyo Disney Resort.

Sights	100–105
Excursions	106

Top 25 TOP 25

Odaiba ▷ **100**
Rikugien Garden ▷ **102**
Tokyo Disney Resort ▷ **103**

URAWA
Urawa
KAWAGUCHI
SKYLINER
Rikugien
Garden
Toyota Auto
Salon Amlux
Ikenukuru
Nippori
Mitaka
Asakusa
Ueno
Shinjuku
Takaido
TOKYO
Tokyo
Chofu
Shibuya
National Museum
of Emerging Science
and Innovation
JR NEX
Meguro
Parasitological
Museum
TOKYO MONORAIL
Odaiba
Shinagawa
Hara Museum of
Contemporary Art
Haneda
International
Airport
TOKYO MONORAIL
KAWASAKI
Shin Yokohama

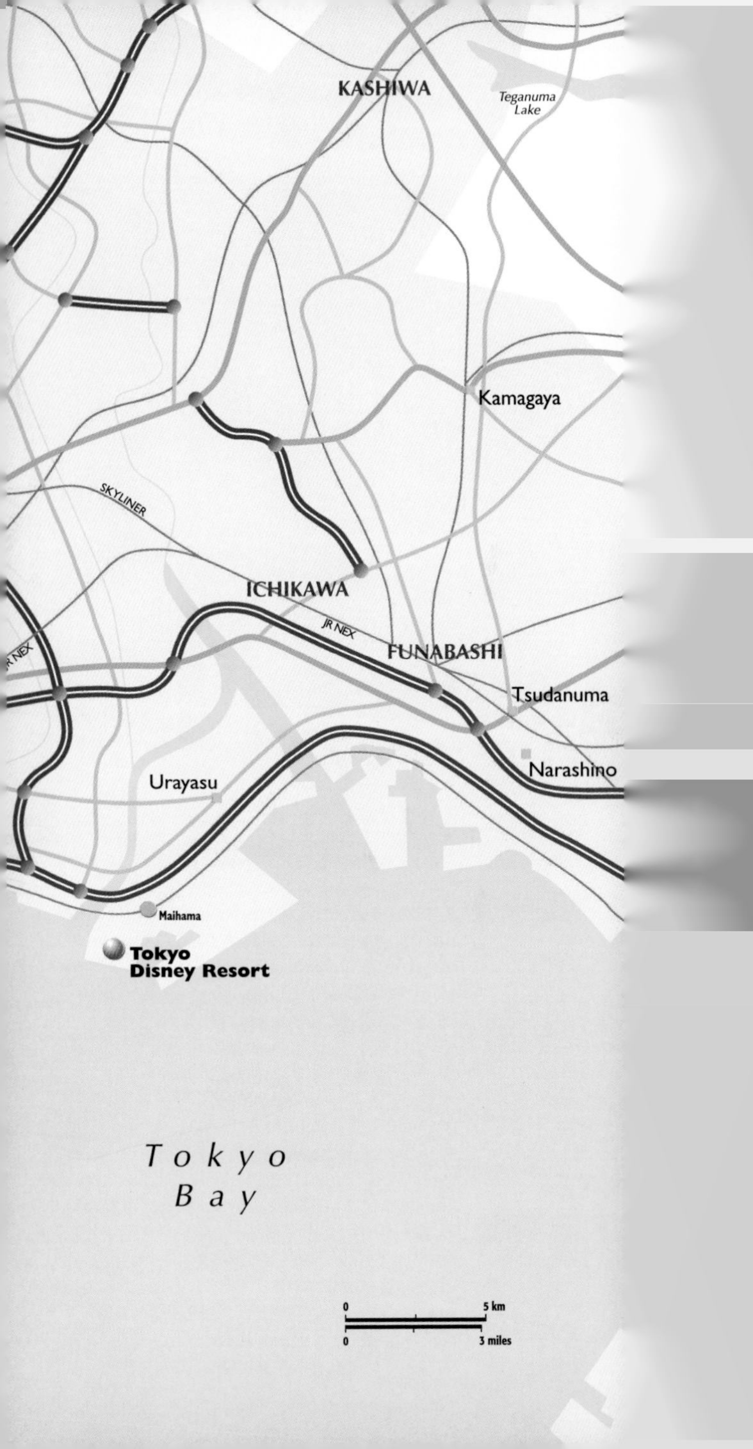

KASHIWA
Teganuma Lake
Kamagaya
SKYLINER
ICHIKAWA
JR NEX
FUNABASHI
Tsudanuma
Narashino
Urayasu
Maihama
Tokyo Disney Resort
Tokyo Bay
0
5 km
0
3 miles

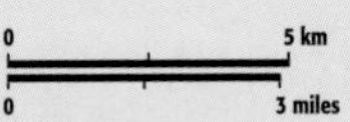

Odaiba

TOP 25

HIGHLIGHTS

- Mega Web
- NeoGeo World
- Giant Sky Wheel
- History Garage
- VenusFort
- Decks Tokyo Beach
- Aqua City/Mediage
- Tokyo Joypolis
- View of Rainbow Bridge

TIP

- This really is a day trip if you include visits to nearby museums.

A vacant stretch of reclaimed land until not long ago, this latest mega development now boasts an amazing collection of entertainment, shopping and exhibition facilities and even its own beach.

Palette Town Start your visit to the complex at Mega Web, a hands-on museum that showcases the latest in automotive technology. Included in the complex is Future World, a glimpse at future transport with a 3-D coaster ride, and a History Garage that displays classic cars from the 1950s to the 1970s. Not far away, you can savor the bay views from the Giant Sky Wheel, the world's largest. The adjoining Sun Walk shopping complex includes restaurants and the women's mega mall, VenusFort, done in 18th-century style, with sculptured fountains and artificial "sky." Check out

Glorious 18th-century European style in the VenusFort mall is an inspiration to shoppers (top and bottom left); the Fuji Television building, which opened in 1997 (right)

the nearby National Museum of Emerging Science and Innovation (▷ 104).

Decks, Joypolis and Seaside Park The Decks shopping and entertainment complex has an array of boutiques and includes the Tokyo Joypolis, a virtual-reality center with thrilling rides and video games. The man-made beach at Seaside Park is popular for sunbathing.

Mediage, Aqua City and Fuji TV headquarters At Mediage, along with cinemas you will find the mini funparks: Where the Wild Things Are, Airtight Garage and the Beatles' Yellow Submarine Adventure. The adjoining Aqua City retail complex has a Toys 'R' Us. Near the Daiba station is the futuristic Fuji Television building with an observation deck, designed by architect Tange Kenzo.

THE BASICS

Off map to southeast
Rinkai-fukutoshin
For information:
Mega Web 3599–0808
VenusFort 3599–0700
Palette Town 3529–1821
Tokyo Joypolis 5500–1801
Aqua City 3599–4700
Mediage 5531–7800
Fuji TV 0180–993–188
Daily 10–10; some vary
Restaurants and cafés
Yurikamome line from Shimbashi station to various stations
Hinode Pier to Odaiba Seaside Park
Good to excellent
Free to expensive
The area is reached via the impressive Rainbow Bridge by train

Rikugien Garden

The inviting entrance to the Rikugien Garden (left); down one of the garden paths (right)

THE BASICS

Off map to north
6-16-3 Honkomagome, Bunkyo-ku
3941-2222
Tue–Sun 9–4.30; closed Dec 29–Jan 3
Komagome
Inexpensive

HIGHLIGHTS

- Historical references
- Literary influences
- Easy walking
- Mountain pass lookout
- Central pond

TIP

- Allow at least two hours to get around the garden.

This delightful Japanese garden, which dates from the late 17th century, is easy to get around, includes an artificial mountain pass and is redolent with geographical and literary references.

A literary garden Widely regarded as the city's most beautiful Japanese garden, Rikugien was laid out in 1695 for a patron with literary tastes: The name is derived from *Rikugi*, the "six forms or principles of classical poetry," and each of its scenic features was inspired by a poetic reference. Cloistered away from the noise of the city by a high wall, this is landscaped art of a high order, entirely artificial yet seemingly perfectly natural.

Historical references Situated in a quiet residential area of northern Tokyo, Rikugien was once in a part of the city where feudal lords lived when they came to Edo, as Tokyo was once called. One of the most influential, Yoshiyasu Yanagisawa, designed this garden, which was seven years in the making. Look out for 88 spots in the garden named after famous Japanese and Chinese places or from episodes from Chinese history. There are also references to a traditional Japanese poetic form known as *waka*.

Charming walks The garden is very accessible for young and old as the paths are mostly level. The large central pond, islands, forested areas, man-made hills and several teahouses all add to the charm. From an artificial mountain pass, you get commanding views of the entire garden.

Adventureland Jungle Cruise (left); Flounder's Flying Fish Coaster (right)

Tokyo Disney Resort

Since its launch in 1983, Tokyo Disneyland Park, modeled on that in California, is as popular as ever. Now, at an adjacent site, Tokyo DisneySea Park features seven ports themed to the myths and legends of the sea.

Disneyland A near replica of the California original, the Tokyo version has all the most popular rides and attractions found in other Disney parks around the world. On busy days, mainly weekends and holidays, you may have to stand in line for half an hour for the popular Big Thunder Mountain, Space Mountain or Star Tours.

DisneySea This consists of attractions, live entertainment, shops and restaurants in theme areas that include: Mediterranean Harbor with its Venetian gondolas; American Waterfront with a transit steamer; Port Discovery with the heart-stopping StormRider; Lost River Delta with a live performance showcasing the rain forest; Arabian Coast, which includes an Arabian Night adventure; Mermaid Lagoon, where kids can ride aboard flying cartoon fish; and Mysterious Island, where you can explore the depths of the ocean with Captain Nemo.

Staying over The five big resort hotels, in the Tokyo Bay area clustered adjacent to the Disney Resort, are perfect for those wishing to take time to explore both parts of the Disney complex.

THE BASICS

www.tokyodisneyresort.co.jp/tdr/index_e
Off map to southeast
1-1 Maihama, Urayasu-shi
0570–00–8632 (English language information)
Open 9am; closing time varies from 7 to 10pm. Closed for six days in mid-Jan
Many restaurants
Urayasu, then bus
Maihama (15 mins from Tokyo station via Keiyo line), then free bus
Very good
Expensive

HIGHLIGHTS

- Space Mountain
- Splash Mountain
- It's a Small World
- Star Tours
- "Fantillusion" evening parade
- Fireworks

TIP

- Try to avoid public or school holidays.

More to See

HARA MUSEUM OF CONTEMPORARY ART
Displays a large collection of abstract Japanese, US and European art from the 1950s to the present day. Housed in an art deco house built by collector Toshio Hara in 1938, the unconventional art is displayed in six galleries. The additional café overlooks pleasant lawns and more outdoor art.
Off map to south 4-7-25 Kita Shinagawa, Shinagawa-ku 3445–0651 Tue–Sun 11–5 (also Wed until 8) Café Shinagawa Expensive

MEGURO PARASITOLOGICAL MUSEUM
The world's only museum of human and animal parasites. The highlight is a 26-ft (7.9-m) tapeworm.
Off map to southwest 4-1-1 Shimo-Meguro, Meguro-ku 3716–1264 Tue–Sun 10–5 Meguro Free

NATIONAL MUSEUM OF EMERGING SCIENCE AND INNOVATION
Seven floors of the very latest scientific technology are displayed with hands-on exhibits as well as events that provide an opportunity to meet scientists. Themes include the environment and technological change, and a dome theater regularly presents topical issues on a spherical screen.
Off map to southeast 2-41-3 Aomi, Koto-ku 3570–9151 Tue–Sun 10–5 Fune-no-Kagakukan (on Yurikamome line) Moderate

TOYOTA AUTO SALON AMLUX
In this futuristic blue steel-and-glass tower, you can climb into every car currently produced by Toyota, inspect the winners of famous Formula 1 races and learn about the latest technical wizardry. There are 70 vehicles on show plus race-car simulators to try out.
Off map to north 3-3-5 Higashi-Ikebukuro, Toshima-ku 5391–5900 Tue–Sun 11–9; closed Tue if Mon is a national holiday Restaurant and snack bar Higashi-Ikebukuro Ikebukuro (7-min walk) Free

Toyota Auto Salon Amlux (above); Giant Sky Wheel at Odaiba (right)

Excursions

THE BASICS

Distance: 54 miles (90km)
Journey Time: 1.5 hours, then local train (55 min)
Open Air Museum daily Mar–Oct 9–5; rest of year 9–4
Hakone-Yumoto (Limited Express from Shinjuku station, Odakyu line)
Expensive

HAKONE

The mountainous area west of Tokyo, with lakes and countless hot springs, is a favorite weekend destination.

From Hakone-Yumoto, the Hakone Tozan Railroad zigzags over the mountains. At Miyanoshita, a resort with thermal pools and mountain walks, stop for lunch or tea at the historic Fujiya Hotel. Next to Chokoku-no-Mori station is Hakone Open Air Museum, a spectacular sculpture garden and gallery. From Gora, a cable car soars over Owakudani Valley, and its sulphurous fumes. Togendai is the base for cruises on Lake Ashi.

THE BASICS

Distance: 30 miles (48km)
Journey Time: About 1 hour
Kita-kamakura or Kamakura from Tokyo station, lower level Track 1 (JR Yokosuka line), or at intermediate stops, Shimbashi or Shinagawa. Hase by local train from Kamakura

KAMAKURA

The samurai ruler Yoritomo Minamoto set up his base at the seaside town of Kamakura in 1192.

Kamakura's many shrines and temples are quite spread out, but you can use the train, which has stops within a short distance of the various temples, to cut down the walking. One of Japan's most important temples, the 13th-century Engakuji Temple, is near to Kita-Kamakura station. The Hase Kannon Temple houses the 37-ft (11.4m) Great Buddha, cast in bronze in 1252.

THE BASICS

Distance: 60 miles (100km)
Journey Time: 2 hours
English-language information line/weather: 0555-72-0259
Kawaguchiko (Odakyu line from Shinjuku station; change at Otsuki)
Tours; buses from Shinjuku to Kawaguchiko

MOUNT FUJI

For most visitors, a view of the perfect volcanic cone is enough, especially as reflected in Lake Ashi.

Gogome is the main starting point for people making the 4- to 5-hour trip to the summit, 12,385ft (3,776m) up. The climb can be made only in July and August, and even then weather can be bad, so be prepared with warm clothing, and always be sure to check the weather conditions before attempting the trek.

Where to Stay

Ryokans offer good basic accommodation and a taste of local culture, while mid-range and top-class hotels compare with the world's best for comfort and service, and are often located closer to the action.

Introduction	**108**
Budget Hotels	**109**
Mid-Range Hotels	**110–111**
Luxury Hotels	**112**

Introduction

Tokyo has a wide variety of accommodation options, ranging from hotels that rank with the best in the world to *minshuku*, a Japanese version of bed-and-breakfast.

Major Hotels

Hotels of all descriptions are located throughout the city, but those establishments near the central area are obviously the most desirable. The best areas and those with most major hotels are Akasaka, Ginza, Shimbashi, Shinjuku and around Tokyo station. The service is invariably first class and they offer a wide range of extras. The Japan Hotel Association has its own website for reservations and information at www.j-hotel.or.jp.

Traditional Japanese Accommodations

Ryokans are traditional Japanese inns, usually two- or three-floor wooden buildings with inner gardens, simple but elegant rooms and flawless service. Rooms normally have tatami (mats) and futon bedding (a thin mattress and quilt), which are rolled up until evening. They are generally a costly way of experiencing Japanese culture and food, although there are some inexpensive versions. Visit www.japaneseguest houses.com for information and reservations. *Minshuku* offer Japanese home-style accommodations. These are a good option for travelers on a budget and for those who wish to gain an insight into the Japanese way of life.

Futon beds, stylish futuristic inte and relaxing baths are characte features of Tokyo accommodatio

OTHER OPTIONS

Capsule hotels accommodate you in stacked boxes, often likened to coffins. At about 3ft x 3ft x 6ft (1m x 1m x 2m), they are not for sufferers of claustrophobia. "Love hotels" give couples a chance to be alone together–their success is a direct result of a lack of living space for Tokyoites who often share space with extended families. Rooms are usually rented by the hour, or two; after 10pm an economy all-night rate applies. Love hotels tend to be concentrated in the entertainment districts such as Shibuya, Ikebukuro, East Shinjuku or Roppongi. Photos of room types are often displayed at the entrance (or in the lobby).

Budget Hotels

PRICES

Expect to pay under ¥12,000 for a double room per night in a budget hotel.

ASIA CENTER OF JAPAN

A rare budget hotel, with 172 plain, Western-style rooms, some with a private bath. Cafeteria. Reserve well in advance. F6 8-10-32 Akasaka, Minato-ku 3402–6111; fax 3402–0738 Aoyama-itchome

CAPSULE HOTEL RIVERSIDE

www.asakusa-capsule.jp/english/

A one-minute walk from the Asakusa station, this hotel has a female-only floor, separate public baths for both men and women, and some kitchen facilities. M2 2-20-4 Kaminarimon, Taito-ku 3844–1157 Asakusa

KIKUYA RYOKAN

A clean, friendly, small inn, with eight tatami rooms, located 10 minutes away from the Senso-ji temple. M2 2-18-9 Nishi-Asakusa, Taito-ku 3841–4051; fax 3841–6404 Tawara-machi

KIMI RYOKAN

www.kimi-ryokan.jp

This friendly little place with 35 Japanese-style rooms is popular with Westerners and often full. It's a seven-minute walk northwest of Ikebukuro station. Off map to north 2-36-8 Ikebukuro, Toshima-ku 3971–3766; fax 3987–1326 Ikebukuro

RYOKAN KATSUTARO

www.katsutaro.com

A short walk from Ueno Park, this small, family-friendly ryokan has seven tatami rooms, laundry facilities, and free internet access. J1/K2 4-16-8 Ikenohata, Taito-ku 3821–9808, fax 3821–4789 Nezu or Ueno

RYOKAN SHIGETSU

www.shigetsu.com

This popular ryokan has separate traditional Japanese baths for men and women overlooking the five-story pagoda. There is internet access in every room, and free internet service in the lobby. M2 1-31-11 Asakusa, Taito-ku 3843–2345; fax 3843–2348 Asakusa

HOSTELS

Expensive by international standards, hostels are often full. Try to reserve well in advance. There's no age restriction, but if you don't belong to any Youth Hostel Association you may be charged extra.

Tokyo international Youth Hostel

Simple dormitory-style accommodations in a modern tower-block. Advance reservations required. 33 rooms. G3 Central Plaza 18F, 1-1 Kaguragashi, Shinjuku-ku 3235–1107; fax 3267–4000 Iidabashi (west exit)

SAKURA HOTEL

www.sakura-hotel.co.jp

A two-minute walk from Jimbocho station, this hotel is within walking distance of the Imperial Palace and the Tokyo Dome. Every room has free internet access, air-conditioning, and TV. J3 2-21-4 Kanda-Jimbocho, Chiyoda-ku 3261–3939; fax 3264–2777 Jimbocho

SAWANOYA RYOKAN

www.sawanoya.com

A modern inn with 12 Japanese-style rooms, close to Ueno Park in the old Yanaka neighborhood. Free internet. J1 2-3-11 Yanaka, Taito-ku 3822–2251; fax 3822–2252 Nezu

YMCA ASIA YOUTH CENTER

Both sexes are welcome. Fifty-five rooms, some with private bath. Seven or eight minutes on foot from Suidobashi or Jimbocho stations. J3 2-5-5 Sarugakucho, Chiyoda-ku 3233–0611; fax 3233–0633 Suidobashi Jimbocho

Mid-Range Hotels

PRICES

Expect to pay between ¥12,000 and ¥25,000 per night for a double room in a mid-range hotel.

AKASAKA YOKO HOTEL

www.yokohotel.co.jp/english/index.html

A few minutes' walk from Akasaka station, this comfortable hotel has free internet access in some rooms, no-smoking rooms on floor 9, and a restaurant that serves both European and Japanese meals.

G6 6-14-12 Akasaka, Minato-ku 3586–4050; fax 3586–5944 Akasaka

ARCA TORRE

www.arktower.co.jp

Roppongi Hills is five minutes away and there are plenty of nightclubs and restaurants in the district. Payment must be made in advance. No triple rooms available.

F7 6-1-23 Roppongi, Minato-ku 3404–5111; fax 3404–5115 Roppongi

ATAMISO

This hotel is close to Ginza's shopping and nightlife. Friendly, personal service with 74 rooms.

J6 4-14-3 Ginza, Chuo-ku 3541–3621; fax 3541–3263 Ginza

CROWNE PLAZA METROPOLITAN

Three minutes' walk from Ikebukuro station, this 815-room well-appointed hotel has a gym and pool.

Off map to northwest 1-6-1 Nishi-Ikebukuro, Toshima-ku 3980–1111; fax 3980–8505 Ikebukuro

GINZA CAPITAL HOTEL

www.ginza-capital.co.jp/en

A basic business hotel with 574 compact rooms, close to Tsukiji subway station, reasonably convenient to Ginza.

K6 3-1-5 Tsukiji, Chuo-ku 3543–8211; fax 3543–7839 Tsukiji

GINZA NIKKO

www.nikkohotels.com

While the 112 rooms may be small, the location, not far from central Ginza, makes this the shopper's choice of accommodations.

J7 8-4-21 Ginza, Chuo-ku 3571–4911; fax 3571–8379 Shimbashi

HOTEL IBIS

www.ibis-hotel.com/

A business hotel with 182 rooms and above average style close to Roppongi. Usually busy at weekends.

F7 7-14-4 Roppongi, Minato-ku 3403–4411; fax 3479–0609 Roppongi

THE BARE ESSENTIALS

Many places in the mid-range category are "business hotels," providing a small room and tiny bathroom, telephone, TV and perhaps an in-house restaurant. The main difference between these and other hotels is their good location. Facilities vary, but most offer internet access and room service.

HOTEL METS SHIBUYA

www.hotelmets.jp/shibuya/

Convenient and well furnished, but be sure to ask for a quiet room on the side away from the busy street. Free internet access and buffet breakfast.

D7 3-29-17 Shibuya, Shibuya-ku 3409–0011; fax 3409–0023 Shibuya

HOTEL PARKSIDE

www.parkside.co.jp

Across from the lotus-filled Shinobazu Pond, this hotel has both European and Japanese-style rooms for all budgets and three restaurants.

K2 2-11-18 Ueno, Taito-ku 3836–5711; fax 3831–6641 Ueno

HOTEL STRIX TOKYO

With larger than usual rooms and free internet access, this European-style hotel is close to the subway and Ikebukuro's huge shopping complexes.

Off map to northwest 2-3-1 Ikebukuro, Toshima-ku 5396–011; fax 5396–9815 Ikebukuro

HOTEL UNIZO SHIMBASHI

www.hotelunizo.com/eng/index.html

A central-area business hotel, a three-minute

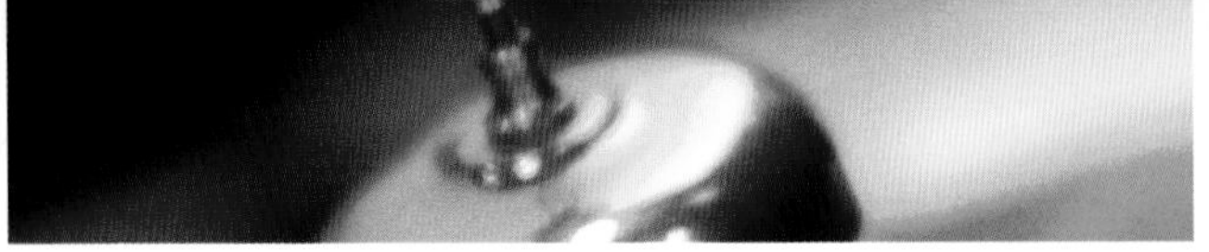

walk from Shimbashi JR or subway stations, one stop away from central Ginza. 233 rooms.
J7 3-5-2 Shimbashi, Minato-ku 3591–3351; fax 3592–1977 Shimbashi

MITSUI URBAN

The orange facade and metal tree sculpture outside have made this clean and efficient hotel a local landmark. Restaurants and internet access in each room.
J7 8-6-15 Ginza, Chuo-ku 3572–4131; fax 3572–4254 Shimbashi

PRESIDENT HOTEL

www.president-hotel.co.jp
The only small, moderately priced hotel in the expensive Aoyama district. Rooms are equipped to a high standard and the restaurants are recommended. Free high-speed internet.
F6 2-2-3 Minami-Aoyama, Minato-ku
3497–0111; fax 3401–4816
Aoyama-Itchome

ROPPONGI PRINCE

www.princehotels japan.com
Compact 216-room hotel close to Roppongi. Courtyard with a café and swimming pool.
F7 3-2-7 Roppongi, Minato-ku 3587–1111; fax 3587–0770 Roppongi

SHIBA DAIMON

This friendly hotel, which sees few Western guests, is in the Tokyo Tower area. It has a good Chinese restaurant.
J8 2-3-6 Shiba-Daimon, Minato-ku
3431–3716; fax 3434–5177
Daimon

SHINJUKU NEW CITY HOTEL

www.newcityhotel.co.jp
Your average mid-range hotel with 400 good size rooms. Just to the west of Shinjuku station.
C4 4-31-1 Nishi-Shinjuku, Shinjuku-ku
3375–651; fax 3375–6535
Tocho-mae

SHINJUKU WASHINGTON

A shiny, modern business hotel near the Shinjuku skyscrapers, with 1,310 compact rooms and largely impersonal or automated services. It is a five-minute walk from Shinjuku station.
D4 3-2-9 Nishi-Shinjuku, Shinjuku-ku
3343-3111 Shinjuku

CHILDREN'S HOTEL

The Children's Castle Hotel is a family-friendly hotel that is part of a huge recreational facility for children in the Aoyama area, although it welcomes travelers without children as well. The hotel has the city's best indoor/outdoor playground for children.
D7 5-53-1 Jingumae, Shibuya-ku 3797–5677; fax 3406–7805; www.kodomonoshiro.or.jp/english/hotel/index.html Shibuya

STAR HOTEL TOKYO

A small, functional but friendly hotel with 80 rooms, a two-minute walk from Shinjuku station and the entertainment district.
D4 7-10-5 Nishi-Shinjuku, Shinjuku-ku
3361–1111; fax 3369–4216
Shinjuku

TOKIWA RYOKAN SHINKAN

A good value ryokan-style hotel with character. It has Western and Japanese rooms, and is well placed in the heart of Shinjuku.
D4 7-27-9 Shinjuku, Shinjuku-ku 3202–4321
Shinjuku

TOKYO STATION

An old-fashioned hotel in part of the historic station building, completed in 1914. Of the 170 rooms, 56 have a bath.
J5 1-9-1 Marunouchi, Chiyoda-ku 3231–2511; fax 3231–3513 Tokyo

YAESU FUJIYA

www.yaesufujiya.com
Modern business hotel behind Tokyo station. The rooms are small but the restaurants are excellent.
J5 2-9-1 Yaesu, Chuo-ku 3273–2111; fax 3273–2180 Tokyo

Luxury Hotels

Expect to pay over ¥25,000 per night for a double room at a luxury hotel.

ANA INTERCONTINENTAL TOKYO

www.anaintercontinental-tokyo.jp/e/

A 37-story, 903-room block with a sober exterior and lots of marble in the Ark Hills area, between Roppongi and Akasaka. Health club, pool, executive floor and restaurants.

G6 1-12-33 Akasaka, Minato-ku 3505–1111; fax 3505–1155 Tameike-Sanno

ASAKUSA VIEW HOTEL

www.viewhotels.co.jp/asakusa/english

Although this is the only hotel with international facilities in this district, it still manages to retain a Japanese feel. Facilities include a Japanese garden, a gym and a swimming pool.

M3 3-17-1 Nishi-Asakusa, Taito-ku 3847–1111; fax 3842–2117 Kuramae

HOTEL NEW OTANI

www.newotani.co.jp/en/

One of Tokyo's very best. There are many stores and more than 30 restaurants, including a revolving buffet restaurant on the 17th floor. The hotel has 1,600 rooms.

G6 4-1 Kioicho, Chiyoda-ku 3265–1111; fax 3221–2619 Akasaka-mitsuke

HOTEL NIKKO TOKYO

This waterfront urban resort, part of the Tokyo Bay area redevelopment (▷ 100), has 453 harbor-view rooms, 8 restaurants, 2 bars and a pool.

Off map to south 1-9-1 Daiba, Minato-ku 5500–5500; fax 5500–2525 Daiba (Yurikamome line)

HOTEL OKURA TOKYO

www.hotelokura.co.jp

This is one of the first of the postwar grand hotels, with 858 rooms, restaurants, an art gallery, and indoor and outdoor pools.

H6 2-10-4 Toranomon, Minato-ku 3582–0111; fax 3582–3707 Toranomon

HOTEL SEIYO GINZA

www.seiyo-ginza.com

In the heart of the Ginza district, this exclusive hotel offers spacious baths, a fitness room and four excellent restaurants.

K5 1-11-2 Ginza, Chuo-ku 3535–1111; fax 3535–1110 Kyobashi

LOST IN TOKYO

Fans of *Lost in Translation* could check out the Park Hyatt Tokyo, where much of the film's story took place. A visit to the New York Bar for a nighttime drink is like stepping onto the movie set.

IMPERIAL HOTEL

www.imperialhotel.co.jp

A city-within-a-city, with easy access to Ginza and facing Hibiya Park. The 1,059 rooms are beautifully appointed. More than 20 restaurants, stores, a health club and pool.

J6 1-1-1 Uchisaiwaicho, Chiyoda-ku 3504–1111; fax 3581–9146 Hibiya

PARK HYATT TOKYO

www.parkhyatttokyo.com

On the 39th to 52nd floors of a pyramid-topped glass tower at the western edge of Shinjuku. It has 178 rooms, 3 restaurants and a pool.

D4 3-7-1-2 Nishi-Shinjuku, Shinjuku-ku 5322–1234; fax 5322–1288 Shinjuku

TOKYO PRINCE HOTEL

www.princehotelsjapan.com

Large rooms, a splendid location, top facilities and attentive service at this 484-room luxury hotel.

H7 3-3-1 Shiba Koen, Minato-ku 3432–1111; fax 3434–5551 Onarimon

WESTIN TOKYO

www.westin.com/tokyo

A stylish hotel with richly decorated public areas and 445 rooms, part of an entertainment and shopping complex.

E9 Yebisu Garden Place, 1-4-1 Mita, Meguro-ku 5423–7000; fax 5423–7600 Ebisu

The information provided on these pages will help you make the most of your trip. Plan your visit, perhaps, to coincide with spring blossom time, the March Doll Festival or the Sumida River Fireworks.

Planning Ahead	**114–115**
Getting There	**116–117**
Getting Around	**118–119**
Essential Facts	**120–122**
Language	**123**
Timeline	**124–125**

Planning Ahead

When to Go

Spring is the best time to visit the city, when the blossoms are at their finest; the fall colors are also beautiful. Both are peak holiday times for the Japanese, and the Golden Week (Apr 29–May 5) is very busy. The monsoon season begins in June. Some attractions close Dec 28–Jan 3.

TIME

Japan is 13 hours ahead of New York, 16 hours ahead of Los Angeles and 9 hours ahead of London GMT.

AVERAGE DAILY MAXIMUM TEMPERATURES

JAN	FEB	MAR	APR	MAY	JUN	JUL	AUG	SEP	OCT	NOV	DEC
48°F	48°F	53°F	65°F	72°F	77°F	84°F	86°F	79°F	70°F	61°F	53°F
9°C	9°C	12°C	18°C	22°C	25°C	29°C	30°C	26°C	21°C	16°C	12°C

Spring (Mar to May) has generally mild days, athough May can be very warm.
Summer (June to August) is hot and humid–maximum 89°F (32°C)–with monsoons in June, bringing rain for days on end.
Fall (September to November) usually brings clear skies and comfortable temperatures. The typhoon season is mid-September to October.
Winter (December to February) is quite dry and not excessively cold–temperatures rarely drop below freezing. The days are usually brisk and bright, and there are occasional light snowfalls.

WHAT'S ON

January *Dezomeshiki* (Jan 6): Acrobatic displays on Chuo-dori, Harumi.
Young Adults' Day: Tens of thousands of 20-year-olds troop to the Meiji Shrine.
February *Setsubun Bean-Throwing Festival* (Feb 3): Held at many shrines and temples to drive away evil.
March *Doll Festival.* Prayers are offered for the well-being of young girls.
May *Sanja Matsuri*: Three-day festival in mid-month with parades of portable shrines at Asakusa Kannon (Sensoji) Temple.
June *Sanno Matsuri* (Jun 10–16)*:* At Hie Jinja, parades carry shrines through Akasaka.
July *Sumida River Fireworks*: First held in 1773, this is Japan's biggest pyrotechnics display.
August *O-Bon*: Buddhist temple festivals honor the ancesters with dancing, fire-works and floating lanterns.
October *Oeshiki Festival* (Oct 11–13): Night lantern procession at Honmonji Buddhist Temple.
November *Emperor Meiji's birthday festival* (Nov 3).
Shichi-go-san (Nov 15): Three-, five- and seven-year old children are taken to shrines.
December *Gishi-sai* (evening of Dec 14): Honors the 47 *ronin* at Sengakuji Temple.
Hagoita-ichi (Dec 17–19): Traditional battledore fair and market at Asakusa Kannon (Sensoji) Temple.
Emperor's Birthday (Dec 23): The Imperial Palace grounds are open.
New Year holiday (Dec 28–Jan 3): Businesses close, along with some attractions.

Tokyo Online

At the heart of Japan's digital culture, Tokyo has an array of English-language websites with regularly updated information on everything from the theater to local news, dining, weather and gossip.

www.tcvb.or.jp/en/index_en.htm
The Tokyo Convention and Visitors Bureau's excellent site, with transportation, attractions, festivals, museums and shopping.

www.bento.com/tokyofood.html
The Tokyo Food Page is a complete guide to eating in Tokyo and Japanese cuisine, with recipes and more than 1,000 restaurant listings.

www.tokyoessentials.com
All you need to help plan your Tokyo trip.

www.planettokyo.com
Guides you through the culture shock of this diverse city.

www.tokyo.to
The online edition of the English-language Tokyo Journal covers art, movies, music, nightlife, dining and events in the city.

www.jnto.go.jp/
The Japanese National Tourist Organization's site with sensible tips on a stay in the city.

www.japan-guide.com
Articles on Japanese life, the economy, history, entertainment and sports.

www.tourism.metro.tokyo.jp/english
Local government site with tips on self-guiding touring, events and public transportation.

www.weekender.co.jp
An online newspaper which includes information on entertainment, art, exhibitions and dining.

USEFUL TRAVEL SITES

www.fodors.com
You can book air tickets, cars and rooms; research prices and weather; pose questions to fellow travelers; and get links to other sites.

www.narita-airport.or.jp
The Narita Airport website details flight arrivals and departures, tourist information and what to expect from airport shopping.

CYBERCAFÉS

Cafe J Net New
✉ 7F Saito Building, 34-5 Udagawacho, Shibuya-ku ☎ 5458–5935
Daily 24 hours
¥600 per hour

Kinkos
✉ 3-9-9 Shibuya, Shibuya-ku ☎ 5464–3391
Daily 24 hours
¥500 per 30 min

Getting There

ENTRY REQUIREMENTS

Citizens of the US, Canada, Netherlands, Australia and New Zealand may stay 90 days without a visa. Citizens of the UK, Republic of Ireland and Germany do not need a visa for stays of up to 180 days. If you do need a visa, your passport must be valid for three months after your entry date.
Foreign nationals entering Japan are required to be photographed and electronically fingerprinted as part of immigration procedures.

AIRPORTS

Narita, Tokyo's international airport, is 40 miles (64km) northeast of the city, served by trains, coaches and taxis. Haneda (12 miles/20km south of the city) is used by domestic flights and China Airlines flights to and from Taiwan.

CAR RENTAL

Experienced international drivers may consider car rental in Japan. Driving is on the left and an International Driving Permit (issued in your country) is required. You can obtain a copy of Rules of the Road from the Japan Automobile Federation at www.jaf.or.jp/e/index.htm. Be aware that while most major destinations are well signposted in English, in rural areas this may not be so.
Be sure to acquire a reliable English–Japanese road atlas before you depart.

- **Hertz – Tokyo**
  www.hertz.com
  ☎ 0120–489–882
- **Nippon Rent-A-Car**
  www.nipponrentacar.co.jp/english/index.html
  ☎ 3485–7196

ARRIVING BY AIR

Narita International Airport (☎ 0476 34-5000) has extensive Japanese and Western dining, and shopping for souvenirs, cameras, electrical and fashion goods. There are two duty-free stores in Terminal 1 and four in Terminal 2.

Airport Limousine coaches (☎ 3665-7220; www.limousinebus.co.jp) run from Narita Airport to Tokyo City Air Terminal (TCAT) and to major hotels (journey time around 90 minutes; ¥3,000; pick-up outside terminals).

Japan Railways (JR) trains connect the airport with Tokyo rail station (55 minutes; ¥2,940) and Shinjuku, said to be the world's biggest and busiest rail station (80 minutes; ¥3,110); the subway stations are adjacent. Keisei Railway trains link the airport to Ueno and Higashi-Ginza subway stations (1 hour; ¥1,920).

Try not to take a taxi—the fare could be as high as ¥30,000, although sharing the cost will help.

A monorail (every 10 minutes) connects

Haneda Airport to Hamamatsu-cho station on the JR Yamanote line (20 minutes; ¥470).

ARRIVING BY BUS

Intercity and regional bus services, operated by numerous companies, terminate and/or pass through Tokyo frequently during the day and at night. Buses are more economical than plane or train if you are prepared to discount the extra time involved due to traffic congestion. JR operates long-distance buses between Tokyo and many major cities.

ARRIVING BY TRAIN

The Japanese railway system is renowned for punctuality and safety. It includes the well-known Japan Railways (JR), a group of six companies which covers the entire country. Of course, the train fare varies depending on the distance you travel and the type of train you catch, such as Limited Express, Express, etc, and the class of reserved seat.

Most travelers will want to travel on the Shinkansen (the "Bullet Trains") and these run regular services between Tokyo and major cities, such as Kyoto, Osaka and Nagoya. Most stations display station names in both Japanese and roman lettering. Tickets for short distances are available from ticket machines at train stations, while long-distance tickets and reservations are handled at the ticket offices of major stations. If there is no English fare chart, buy the cheapest ticket at the vending machine and pay the difference due at the fare adjustment office of your destination station. Most trains stop operating around midnight.

If you are considering lots of rail travel, then buy a Japan Rail Pass for its excellent value and convenience. The pass must be purchased outside of Japan, so organize it before you enter the country. Holders of this pass are offered hotel discounts at JR Group Hotels.

INSURANCE

Check your coverage before traveling and buy a supplementary policy if needed. Japanese hospitals have high standards but are expensive. No vaccinations are required to enter Japan.

CUSTOMS REGULATIONS

Duty-free allowances are 200 cigarettes or 50 cigars, 3 x 760ml bottles of liquor, 56ml perfume and ¥200,000 worth of gifts.

VISITORS WITH DISABILITIES

Tokyo is not the easiest city for visitors in wheelchairs because the subway system has few elevators or escalators; trains are crowded; and people tend to dash around. But many new buildings have excellent facilities for disabled visitors, and there are some special walkways for sight-impaired pedestrians.

BULKY LUGGAGE

If you are traveling with large suitcases, you might consider using airport delivery or "takkyubin" services. There are counters at the airport arrival lounges. For more information, see www.japan-guide.com/e/e2278.html and www.narita-airport.jp/en/guide/service

Getting Around

WHERE TO GET MAPS

- Larger hotels give out excellent city and subway maps; large stations supply subway maps.
- For both leaflets and maps, visit the Tourist Information Centers (TICs) run by JNTO at ✉ Narita Airport Terminal 2, and in the city center at ✚ J6 ✉ 10F Tokyo Kotosukaikan Building, 2-10-1 Yurakucho, Chiyoda-ku ☎ 3201–3331 ⏲ Mon–Fri 9–5, Sat 9–noon; closed Dec 29–Jan 1 Ⓜ Yurakucho
- TTIC ✚ C4 ✉ Tokyo Metropolitan Government Building (Main Building No 1, 1F) 8-1, Nishi-Shinjuku 2-chome, Shinjuku-ku ☎ 5321–3077 ⏲ Daily 9.30–6.30; closed Dec 29–Jan 1 Ⓜ Tochomae

LOST PROPERTY

- **Tokyo Metro** ☎ 3834–5577; TOEI lines ☎ 3812–2011
- **JR trains** ☎ 3231–1880 (Tokyo station) ☎ 3841–8069 (Ueno station)
- **Taxis** ☎ 3648–0300
- **Buses** ☎ 3818–5760

Tokyo has an excellent public transportation system, consisting of efficient subway, rail and bus networks.

BUSES

- Public buses are slower and more confusing than the subway. Destinations, and information at stops, are usually marked only in Japanese characters.
- Make sure you know the route number, and it is best to have your destination written down in Japanese to show people when asking for help.
- On boarding, passengers take a numbered ticket. The fare is shown on an electronic display and paid on leaving the bus.

THE METRO

- The subway (Metro) is the usual way of getting around in Tokyo but can be very crowded at peak periods. The JR Yamanote rail loop line links important central locations and can be quicker than the subway. Pick up a map of the system at major stations. Each line is identified by a color, used consistently on maps, signs and sometimes on the trains, too. EIDAN and TOEI Metro lines and JR one-day tickets allow unlimited travel but seldom pay for themselves. Purchase a JR iO card and a subway Pass Net to save buying tickets. High-denomination cards yield a small discount. Tickets are not interchangeable between JR, subway and private lines.
- At the station, find the row of ticket machines for the line you want. Price lists are displayed nearby. If you cannot find one, buy the lowest price ticket and pay any extra at your destination at "Fare Adjustment" machines.
- Machines give change.
- Feed the ticket face up into the entry gate and collect it when the machine expels it. It is essential that you keep it until the ride is over.
- Follow signs to the line and platform (track) you need, sometimes identified by the final station on the line. Stand at the yellow markers

and if there are any passengers on the train, wait to one side before boarding.

- At each stop, signs give the station's name and that of the next in Japanese and Roman script.
- At your destination, find an exit directory (a yellow board); note the number of the exit you want before going through the ticket gate.
- Travel light at rush hour. There are many stairs, and long walks to exits or when you are transferring between lines.

TAXIS

- It is best to show an area map with your destination marked.
- Taxis charge a high rate for the first 2km (just over 1 mile), ¥670 (and 30 percent more from 11pm to 5am). The fare then rises rapidly. A red light in the front window indicates that a taxi is available. Use the left-hand, curbside door; it opens and closes by remote control. Don't try to do it yourself.
- Pay only the fare on the meter. Tipping is not expected.

TRAINS

- The rail system, a mix of the government JR companies and several private lines, offers regular services, is spotlessly clean and runs on time. Rail staff are generally very helpful.
- The JR has an English-language telephone service (☎ 3423-0111).
- www.japanrail.com is useful in preparing for rail travel in Japan.
- www.japanrailpass.net has information on the most economical way to travel throughout Japan by rail (▷ 117).

WALKING

- Walking is the best way to discover specialty shops and restaurants in out-of-the-way back-streets.
- Don't worry about getting lost; almost anyone you ask, pointing to your destination on a map, will provide you with directions.

FINDING AN ADDRESS

- Few streets have names, and when they do, these are rarely used in addresses. Even taxi drivers have trouble.
- Building numbers generally relate to the order of construction, not to position.
- In a Tokyo address such as 3-10-2 Akasaka (the district), Minato-ku (city ward), 3 is the subdivision or "chome", 10 is the block or "ban" and 2 the number or "go." 'F' means floor; ground level is 1F.
- A map pinpointing the place and related landmarks is essential.

DRIVING IN TOKYO

While driving within Tokyo city is not recommended due to congestion and parking problems, driving on major roads between cities is a viable alternative to public transportation.

Tokyo has an extensive system of freeways, but tolls are high. Remember, traffic keeps to the left.

SENSIBLE PRECAUTIONS

- Tokyo is the safest of the world's big cities to walk around–even in the raunchier areas, such as Kabukicho.
- Use hotel safes for storing large sums of money.
- Streets and subways are safe but always exercise caution if walking at night.

Essential Facts

EMBASSIES

- Australia ✉ 2-1-14 Mita, Minato-ku ☎ 5232–4111
- Canada ✉ 7-3-38 Akasaka, Minato-ku ☎ 5412–6200
- Germany B4-5-10 Minami-Azabu ☎ 3473–0151
- Netherlands ✉ 3-6-3 Shiba Koen, Minato-ku ☎ 5401–0411
- UK ✉ 1 Ichiban-cho, Chiyoda-ku ☎ 5211–1100
- USA ✉ 1-10-5 Akasaka, Minato-ku ☎ 3224–5000

MONEY

The unit of currency is the yen (¥). Coins in use are ¥1, ¥5, ¥10, ¥50, ¥100 and ¥500. Bank-notes are for ¥1,000, ¥2,000, ¥5,000 and ¥10,000.

1,000 yen

2,000 yen

5,000 yen

10,000 yen

ELECTRICITY

- 100V AC, 50Hz. US 110V equipment will operate. Plugs have two flat, parallel pins.

EMERGENCY PHONE NUMBERS

- Police ☎ 110
- Fire and Ambulance ☎ 119
- Emergency numbers are toll-free. On pay phones push the red button first.

ETIQUETTE

- Japanese custom is to bow when meeting someone. A handshake will be accepted, but an attempt to follow custom and give a bow will be appreciated.
- When visiting a Japanese home, bring a present, ideally something from your own country.
- Shoes must be removed before entering a home, a ryokan, many shrine halls and some restaurants. Slippers are usually provided, but it will save embarrassment if your socks are free from holes.
- Visiting cards are exchanged at every opportunity. If you are on business, take a large supply. They should state your position in your organization. If possible, have a translation in Japanese characters printed on the reverse. Hotels can arrange this quickly. When given a card, study it with interest; do not put it away unread.
- For table etiquette (▷ panels, 81, 82).
- It is not usual to tip in Japan, except for special extra services. A 10–15 percent service charge is added to hotel and some restaurant bills. Porters charge a set fee.

MEDIA

- A full range of foreign magazines is stocked at newsstands in big hotels and major train stations and in large bookstores.
- The quarterly *Tokyo Journal* has full listings of exhibitions, markets, services and entertainment. Restaurant, club and bar reviews may be biased to advertisers.

● There are four English-language translations of the main Japanese dailies: the *Japan Times*, *Daily Yomiuri*, *Mainichi Daily News* and *Asahi Evening News*.

MONEY MATTERS

● Traveler's checks in yen may be used instead of cash. Those in other currencies can be changed at banks or at hotels, where the exchange rate may not be quite as good. A passport is needed.

● Major credit cards are accepted by most hotels, big stores and many restaurants, but rarely by smaller ones or fast-food outlets. It is still essential, and safe, to carry cash. Telephones and ticket-vending machines take 10, 50 and 100 yen coins.

● ATMs outside banks will take some cards. Check with card issuers for details.

NATIONAL HOLIDAYS

● If a national holiday falls on a Sunday, the Monday following is a holiday.

● January 1: New Year's Day;
Second Monday in January: Coming of Age Day for 20-year-olds.

● February 11: Foundation Day.

● March 20 or 21: Vernal Equinox Day.

● April 29: Showa Day.

● May 3: Constitution Day; 4: Greenery Day; 5: Children's Day.

● Third Monday of September: Respect for the Aged Day;
22 or 23: Autumn Equinox Day.

● Second Monday of October: Health and Sports Day.

● November 3: Culture Day; 23: Labour Day.

● 23 December: Emperor's Birthday.

PLACES OF WORSHIP

The following have services in English:

● Roman Catholic: Franciscan Chapel Center ✉ 4-2-37 Roppongi, Minato-ku ☎ 3401–2141

● Protestant: Tokyo Bapist ✉ 9-2 Hachiya-macho, Shibuya-ku ☎ 3461–8425

OPENING HOURS

● Shops: Mon–Sat 10–6, 7 or 8

● Banks: Mon–Fri 9–3

● Offices: Mon–Fri 9–5 (some businesses work half day on Sat)

● Museums: Tue–Sun 10, 10.30 or 11–4 or 5. (Closed Tue if Mon is a national holiday.)

POST OFFICES

● Hotel desks are the most convenient places to post letters and cards. They have stamps and are familiar with postal rates.

● Go to post offices only to send heavy packages or registered mail. Staff can read Roman script.

● Post offices open Mon–Fri 9–5

● Tokyo Central Post Office ✉ 2-7-2 Marunouchi, Chiyoda-ku ☎ 3284–9602 ⏲ Mon–Fri 9–9, Sat, Sun and public holidays 9–7

• Jewish: Jewish Community Centre ✉ 3-8-8 Hiroo, Shibuya-ku ☎ 3400–2559
• Islamic: Tokyo Mosque ✉ 1-19 Oyama-cho, Shibuya-ku ☎ 5790–0760
• Interdenominational: Tokyo Union Church ✉ 5-7-7 Jingu-mae, Shibuya-ku ☎ 3400–0047

TELEPHONES

• Coin- and card-operated phones are prevalent. Local calls cost ¥10 per minute. ¥500 or ¥1,000 cards are sold at hotels, airports, station kiosks and machines near phones.
• Make international direct-dial calls from gray and green phones with a gold front panel, card phones, or phones marked "international." Use only ¥100 coins, or cards. Several companies compete, each having its own international access code. Dial 0057 (for KDDI), 0088-41 (ITJ) or 0061 (SoftBank), followed by the country code, area code (omit any initial 0) and number. The calling card codes of other international companies can also be used. MCI ☎ 0039–121 or 0066–55–121; AT&T ☎ 0039–111 or 0066-55–111
• The area code for central Tokyo is 03.
• 0120 is a toll-free dialing number
• Dial 0051 for person-to-person and collect (reverse charge) calls, and 0057 (toll-free) for information.
• Mobile phones from other countries are not compatible with Japanese networks.

TOILETS

• Hotels have the Western type; some even an optional "paperless" mode with warm water jets and hot air to clean your underside.
• The Japanese version, in most public toilets, is at ground level with no seat. You squat over it, facing the flushing handle. It is a good idea to carry your own toilet paper.
• Department stores usually provide both versions for their customers.

MEDICAL TREATMENT

• Standards–and costs–are high.
• Your embassy can recommend hospitals with some doctors who speak English.
• International Medical Information Center Toyko ☎ 5285–8088

MEDICATION

• For prescription and nonprescription medication, when you need an English speaker: American Pharmacy ✚ K6 ✉ Hibiya Park Building, 1-8-1 Yurakucho, Chiyodu-ku ☎ 3271–4034 🕒 Mon–Sat 9–7.30, Sun 10–6.30 Ⓜ Ginza

TIME DIFFERENCES

Time differences between Japan and other major world cities:
Frankfurt – 8hrs behind Japan
London GMT – 9hrs behind
Paris – 8hrs behind
Sydney – 1hr ahead
Chicago – 15hrs behind
Los Angeles – 16hrs behind
New York – 13hrs behind
San Francisco – 16hrs behind
Toronto – 14hrs behind
Bangkok – 2hrs behind
Hong Kong – 1hr behind
Seoul – no time difference
Beijing – 1hr behind

Language

- Romanized versions of Japanese words are more or less phonetic, so say the words as written.
- Give all syllables equal weight, except: "u" at the end of a word, which is hardly sounded at all; "i" in the middle of a word, which is skipped over, as in mash'te for mashite.
- "E" sounds like "eh" in ten; "g" is generally hard, as in go.
- Two adjoining consonants are sounded separately.
- A dash over a vowel (macron; not used in this book) lengthens the vowel sound.
- Family names are now usually written second in English.

USEFUL WORDS AND PHRASES	
How do you do?	*Hajime-mashite*
Good morning	*Ohayo gozai-masu*
Good afternoon	*Kon-nichi-wa*
Good evening	*Konban-wa*
Good night	*Oyasumi-nasai*
Good-bye	*Sayo-nara*
Mr, Mrs, Miss, Ms	*-san* (suffix to family name, or given name of friends)
Thank you	*Domo/arigato*
Excuse me, sorry	*Sumi-masen*
Please (when offering)	*Dozo*
Please (when asking)	*Kudasai*
Hello (telephone)	*Moshi-moshi*
Yes	*Hai*
Do you understand?	*Wakari-masu-ka?*
Do you speak English?	*Eigo o hanashi-masu-ka?*
Where is ...?	*... wa doko desu-ka? (place name first)*

NUMBERS	
1	*ichi*
2	*ni*
3	*san*
4	*yon*
5	*go*
6	*roku*
7	*nana*
8	*hachi*
9	*kyu*
10	*ju*
20	*ni-ju*
30	*san-ju*
40	*yon-ju*
50	*go-ju*
100	*hyaku*
1,000	*sen*

Timeline

THE ENGLISH PILOT

In April 1600, the lone surviving ship of a Dutch trading fleet reached Japan, crewed by a mere six men. One was an English pilot, Will Adams. He was taken to meet Ieyasu, who was eager to learn about European ways and who asked Adams to build him a ship. The pilot ("Anjin-san") spent the rest of his life serving the shoguns, dying in 1620. Readers of James Clavell's novel *Shogun* will recognize the story, although names were changed and many details invented.

250–710 Kofun Culture. From 300 to 400 unification under Yamato clan. Yamato power declines 400–600. Spread of Buddhism.

794 Imperial capital moves from Nara to Kyoto.

850–1150 Rise of the samurai (warrior) class and rapid spread of Buddhism.

1192 *Bushi*, or samurai, are victorious in a power struggle. Yoritomo Minamoto rules from Kamakura as shogun.

1336 Takauji Ashikaga takes over as shogun and establishes his rule in Kyoto.

1572–1600 The warlord Nobunaga Oda seizes power in Kyoto. After Oda is murdered in 1582, Hideyoshi Toyotomi unites the country. On his death in 1598, a power struggle ensues.

1600–39 Ieyasu Tokugawa is victorious at the battle of Sekigahara. The Tokugawa shogunate is established.

1853/58 The Treaty of Kanagawa, signed in 1858, opens ports to trade.

1867–68 A chain of events leads to the installation of the Emperor Meiji. Edo is renamed Tokyo ("Eastern Capital"). Shinto is declared the state religion.

From left: detail of a woodblock print of a samurai warrior; a front piece of the Asakusa Sensoji Kannon Temple (Sensoji Temple) from 1721, with an old protective religious symbol; statue of a Japanese soldier on display in the War Memorial Museum at the Yasukuni shrine

1894–1910 War with China and Russia. In 1910 Japan annexes Korea.

1923 An earthquake in the city kills about 140,000 people.

1926 Hirohito becomes emperor.

1930s The military increasingly dominate the government. Japan invades China.

1945–52 US General Douglas MacArthur rules after Japan surrenders at the end of World War II. Emperor Hirohito renounces his claim to divine status. Japanese independence is restored in 1952.

1960s Rapid economic and industrial recovery. Tokyo hosts Olympic Games in 1964.

1980s Japan becomes the world's greatest trading nation. Tokyo's stock market booms. Emperor Akihito succeeds Hirohito in 1989.

1991–94 Recession. The stock market falls by 60 percent.

1995 An earthquake devastates Kobe.

2000 The economy continues to stagnate amid record unemployment and bankruptcies.

2005 Tokyo construction boom.

2008 The economy continues to recover.

WORLD WAR II

In December 1941 Japan attacked Pearl Harbor, and the US entered World War II. Defeat by the US navy in the Battle of Midway marked the turning point of the war. In 1944–45 air raids leveled much of Tokyo. On two nights in March 1945, much of the city was destroyed by fire; around 100,000 died and a million homes were destroyed. Atomic bombs were dropped on Hiroshima (440 miles/708km from Tokyo) and Nagasaki (610 miles/981km from Tokyo) despite Japan's imminent surrender.

From left: bronze statue of celebrated bureaucrat Kiyomaro Wakeno from the late Nara-Haian period, outside the Japan Meteorological Agency building; a Type 52 Zero Fighter plane in the War Memorial Museum at the Yasukuni shrine

Index

A
accommodation 17, 108–112
addresses, finding 119
air travel 116–117
antiques 12, 35, 47, 62
aquarium 74
Asakusa Kannon Temple 8, 86–87
Asakusa-jinja Shrine 87

B
banks 121
beer halls and gardens 16, 17, 36, 63, 95
Beer Museum 46
blossom time 29, 114
Bridgestone Museum of Art 76
bunraku theater 63
buses 117, 118

C
capsule hotels 108
car rental 116
children 17, 111
Chiyoda-ku 51–64
  entertainment and nightlife 63
  map 52–53
  restaurants 64
  shopping 62
  sights 54–60
  walk 61
cinemas 36, 48, 63
climate and seasons 114
credit cards 121
customs regulations 117
cybercafés 115

D
disabilities, visitors with 117
driving 116, 119

E
eating out 14–15
  chopsticks 14, 81, 82
  eating places 14
  etiquette 14, 81, 82
  menu reader 38, 49
  miso soup 64
  sushi 50
  tofu 96
  see also restaurants
Edo-Tokyo Museum 8, 88
electricity 120
electronics 10, 12, 16, 62, 73
embassies 120
emergency phone numbers 120
Engakuji Temple 106
entertainment and nightlife 13, 17, 18
  Chiyoda-ku 63
  Ginza and Around 79
  Roppongi and Around 48
  Shibuya-ku and Shinjuku-ku 36
  Ueno 95
etiquette 5, 14, 81, 82, 120

F
festivals and events 114
fun parks 92, 101, 103

G
gardens and parks
  Hamarikyu Garden 9, 70–71
  Hibiya Park 9, 56, 61
  Imperial Palace East Garden 9, 18, 54–55, 61
  Meiji Jingu Shrine 25
  New Otani Hotel Garden 60
  Rikugien Garden 9, 102
  Shinjuku Gyoen National Garden 8, 18, 28–29
  Ueno Park 93
  Yoyogi Park 24, 33
geishas 13, 79
Ginza 4, 8, 11, 68–69, 77
Ginza and Around 65–82
  entertainment and nightlife 79
  map 66–67
  restaurants 81–82
  shopping 78
  sights 68–76
  walk 77
Grand Prince Akasaka Hotel 60

H
Hakone 106
Hakone Open Air Museum 106
Hamarikyu Garden 9, 70–71
Hanazono Shrine 30
Hara Museum of Contemporary Art 104
Harajuku 4, 9, 24
Hase Kannon Temple 106
Hibiya City 56
Hibiya Park 9, 56, 61
Hie Shrine 60
history 124–125
hostels 109
hot springs 48, 95, 106
hotels 17, 108–112
House of Shiseido 76

I
Idemitsu Museum of Modern Arts 60
Imperial Hotel 56
Imperial Palace East Garden 9, 18, 54–55, 61
insurance 117

J
Japan Folk Crafts Museum 30–31
Japanese Sword Museum 30
Japanese women 5

K
kabuki theater 36, 63, 72
Kabuki-za Theater 9, 17, 72
Kamakura 106
Keio Plaza Hotel 47th Floor 30
Kiyomizu Kannon Temple 92

L
language 123
  menu reader 38, 49
lost property 118
love hotels 108
luggage 117

M
manga (comic books) 10
markets 11, 12, 24, 47, 95
martial arts 63
medical treatment 122
medication 122
Mega Web 100
Meguro Parasitological Museum 104
Meiji Jingu Shrine 9, 25, 34
Metro 118–119
Metropolitan Government Offices 9, 26–27
Miyanoshita 106
money 120, 121
Mori Art Center 42
Mount Fuji 106
museum and gallery opening hours 121
museums and galleries
  Beer Museum 46
  Bridgestone Museum of Art 76
  Edo-Tokyo Museum 8, 88
  Hakone Open Air Museum 106
  Hara Museum of Contemporary Art 104
  Idemitsu Museum of Modern Arts 60
  Japan Folk Crafts Museum 30–31
  Japanese Sword Museum 30
  Mega Web 100
  Meguro Parasitological Museum 104
  Mori Art Center 42
  National Museum of Emerging Science and Innovation 104
  National Museum of Modern Art 9, 58
  National Museum of Western Art 9, 89
  Nezu Institute of Fine Arts 46
  Ota Memorial Museum of Art 31, 34
  Seiji Togo Memorial Art Museum 31
  Shitamachi Museum 92

Sumo Museum 92
TEPCO Electric Energy Museum 32
Tokyo Metropolitan Art Museum 93
Tokyo Metropolitan Museum of Photography 18, 46
Tokyo National Museum 8, 90–91
Treasure Museum 25
Trick Art Gallery 74
War Memorial Museum 59
Watari Museum of Contemporary Art 33

N
National Diet Building 9, 57
national holidays 121
National Museum of Emerging Science and Innovation 104
National Museum of Modern Art 9, 58
National Museum of Western Art 9, 89
National Yoyogi Sports Center and Stadium 33
New Otani Hotel Garden 60
newspapers and magazines 120–121
Nezu Institute of Fine Arts 46
NHK Broadcasting Center 30
night tours 13
Nihon Mingeikan 30–31
noh theater 36, 48
NTT Intercommunication Center 31

O
Odaiba 4, 9, 100–101
Omotesando-dori 4, 34
opening hours 121
Ota Memorial Museum of Art 31, 34

P
passports and visas 116
pharmacies 122
places of worship 121–122
post offices 121
public transport 118–119

R
restaurants 15, 16
Chiyoda-ku 64
Ginza and Around 81–82
Roppongi and Around 49–50
Shibuya-ku and Shinjuku-ku 37–38
Ueno 96
Rikugien Garden 9, 102
river cruise 9, 71
Roppongi and Around 13, 39–50
entertainment and nightlife 48
map 40–41
restaurants 49–50
shopping 47
sights 42–46
Roppongi Hills 4, 9, 18, 42–43
ryokans (Japanese inns) 108

S
safety 119
Seiji Togo Memorial Art Museum 31
Sengakuji Temple 8, 44
Shibuya 13
Shibuya-ku and Shinjuku-ku 20–38
entertainment and nightlife 36
map 22–23
restaurants 37–38
shopping 35
sights 24–33
walk 34
Shinjuku Gyoen National Garden 8, 18, 28–29
Shinjuku station 32
Shinkansen (Bullet Trains) 117
Shitamachi Museum 92
shopping 10–12, 16
Chiyoda-ku 62
Ginza and Around 78
opening hours 121
Roppongi and Around 47
Shibuya-ku and Shinjuku-ku 35
Ueno 95
Sogenji Temple 92
Sony Building 8, 73
Sumitomo Tower 32
Sumiyoshi Shrine 76
Sumo Museum 92
sumo wrestling 92, 95

T
Takeshita-dori 11, 17, 24
taxis 119
telephones 122
temples and shrines
Asakusa Kannon Temple 8, 86–87
Asakusa-jinja Shrine 87
Engakuji Temple 106
Hanazono Shrine 30
Hase Kannon Temple 106
Hie Shrine 60
Kiyomizu Kannon Temple 92
Meiji Jingu Shrine 9, 25, 34
Sengakuji Temple 8, 44
Sogenji Temple 92
Sumiyoshi Shrine 76
Togo Shrine 33
Toshogu Shrine 93
Yasukuni Shrine 8, 59
Zojoji Temple 76
TEPCO Electric Energy Museum 32
ticket agencies 79
time differences 114, 122
tipping 120
Togendai 106
Togo Shrine 33
toilets 122
Tokyo Anime Center 17, 62, 63
Tokyo City View 18, 42
Tokyo Disney Resort 8, 17, 103
Tokyo Dome City 92
Tokyo Metropolitan Art Museum 93
Tokyo Metropolitan Museum of Photography 18, 46
Tokyo National Museum 8, 90–91
Tokyo Opera City 33, 36
Tokyo Tower 8, 18, 74
Toshogu Shrine 93
tourist information 115, 118
Toyota Auto Salon Amlux 104
train services 117, 119
traveler's checks 121
Treasure Museum 25
Trick Art Gallery 74
Tsukiji Fish Market 8, 75, 77
two-day itinerary 6–7

U
Ueno 4, 11, 83–96
entertainment and nightlife 95
map 84–85
restaurants 96
shopping 95
sights 86–93
walk 94
Ueno Park 93, 94
Ueno Zoo 93

V
views of Tokyo 18
visiting cards 120

W
walks
Harajuku to Omotesando 34
Imperial Palace East Garden to Hibiya Park 61
Tsukiji/Ginza 77
Stroll around Ueno 94
War Memorial Museum 59
Watari Museum of Contemporary Art 33
websites 115
Westin Tokyo Hotel 45, 46

Y
Yasukuni Shrine 8, 59
Yebisu Garden Place 8, 18, 45
Yoyogi Park 24, 33

Z
Zojoji Temple 76

Tokyo's
25 Best

WRITTEN BY Martin Gostelow
ADDITIONAL WRITING Rod Ritchie
DESIGN CONCEPT Kate Harling
DESIGN WORK Jacqueline Bailey
COVER DESIGN Tigist Getachew
PROOFREADER Kazumi Pestka
INDEXER Marie Lorimer
IMAGE RETOUCHING AND REPRO Michael Moody, Sarah Montgomery
EDITOR Edith Summerhayes
REVIEWING EDITOR Paul Eisenberg
SERIES EDITORS Paul Mitchell, Edith Summerhayes

Published in the United Kingdom by AA Publishing

ISBN 978-1-4000-1886-4

SIXTH EDITION

IMPORTANT TIP
Time inevitably brings changes, so always confirm prices, travel facts, and other perishable information when it matters. Although Fodor's cannot accept responsibility for errors, you can use this guide in the confidence that we have taken every care to ensure its accuracy.

SPECIAL SALES
This book is available for special discounts for bulk purchases for sales promotions or premiums. Special editions, including personalized covers, excerpts of existing books, and corporate imprints, can be created in large quantities for special needs. For more information, write to Special Markets/Premium Sales, 1745 Broadway, MD 6–2, New York, NY 10019 or email specialmarkets@randomhouse.com.

Color separation by Keenes, Andover, UK
Printed and bound by Leo Paper Products, China
10 9 8 7 6 5 4 3 2 1

A03145
Mapping in this title produced from mapping © MAIRDUMONT / Falk Verlag 2008
and map data supplied by Global Mapping, Brackley, UK. Copyright © Global Mapping/ITMB
Transport map © Communicarta Ltd, UK

The Automobile Association wishes to thank the following photographers, companies and picture libraries for their assistance in the preparation of this book.

This book makes reference to various Disney copyrighted characters, trademarks, marks and registered marks owned by The Walt Disney Company and Disney Enterprises, Inc.

Abbreviations for the picture credits are as follows – (t) top; (b) bottom; (c) centre; (l) left; (r) right; (AA) AA World Travel Library.

1 AA/Mike Langford; **2–18t** AA/Mike Langford; **4cl** AA/Jackie Ranken; **5c–b** AA/Jackie Ranken; **6cl** AA/Mike Langford; **6cc** AA/Mike Langford; **6cr** AA/Mike Langford; **6bl** AA/Jackie Ranken; **6cc** AA/Jackie Ranken; **6cr** AA/Mike Langford; **7cl** AA/Jackie Ranken; **7cc** AA/Jackie Ranken; **7cr** AA/Mike Langford; **7bl** AA/Mike Langford; **7bc** AA/Mike Langford; **7br** AA/Jackie Ranken; **10/11t** AA/Mike Langford; **10cr** AA/Jackie Ranken; **10/11b** AA/Jackie Ranken; **11cl** AA/Mike Langford; **11cl** AA/Jackie Ranken; **12b** AA/Mike Langford; **13ctl** AA/Jackie Ranken; **13cl** AA/Mike Langford; **13bl** AA/Jackie Ranken; **14(i)** AA/Mike Langford; **14(ii)** AA/Jackie Ranken; **14(iii)** AA/Mike Langford; **14(iv)** AA/Mike Langford; **15b** AA/Jackie Ranken; **16(i)** AA/Mike Langford; **16(ii)** AA/Jackie Ranken; **16(iii)** AA/Mike Langford; **16(iv)** AA/Mike Langford; **17(i)** AA/Jackie Ranken; **17(ii)** AA/Mike Langford; **17(iii)** AA/Mike Langford; **17(iv)** AA/Jackie Ranken; **18(i)** AA/Mike Langford; **18(ii)** AA/Jackie Ranken; **18(iii)** AA/Jackie Ranken; **18(iv)** AA/Jackie Ranken; **19(i)** AA/Mike Langford; **19(ii)** AA/Jackie Ranken; **19(iii)** AA/Jackie Ranken; **19(iv)** AA/Mike Langford; **19(v)** AA/Mike Langford; **19(vi)** AA/Jackie Ranken; **20/21** AA/Mike Langford; **24l** AA/Jackie Ranken; **24r** AA/Mike Langford; **25l** AA/Mike Langford; **25r** AA/Mike Langford; **26l** AA/Jackie Ranken; **26tr** AA/Jackie Ranken; **26cr** AA/Jackie Ranken; **27t** AA/Mike Langford; **27c** AA/Mike Langford; **27cr** AA/Mike Langford; **28l** AA/Jackie Ranken; **28/29t** AA/Jackie Ranken; **28cr** AA/Jackie Ranken; **29cr** AA/Mike Langford; **30–33t** AA/Jackie Ranken; **30bl** AA/Jackie Ranken; **30br** AA/Mike Langford; **31bl** AA/Mike Langford; **31br** AA/Mike Langford; **32bl** Paul Chesley/Getty Images; **32br** AA/Jackie Ranken; **33bl** AA/Mike Langford; **33br** AA/Jackie Ranken; **34t** AA/Jackie Ranken; **35t** AA/Jackie Ranken; **36t** AA/Jackie Ranken; **37–38t** AA/Mike Langford; **39** AA/Jackie Ranken; **42tl** AA/Jackie Ranken; **42tr** AA/Jackie Ranken; **43** AA/Mike Langford; **44l** AA/Jackie Ranken; **44c** AA/Mike Langford; **44r** AA/Mike Langford; **45l** AA/Mike Langford; **45r** AA/Jackie Ranken; **46t** AA/Jackie Ranken; **46bl** AA/Mike Langford; **46br** AA/Mike Langford; **47t** AA/Jackie Ranken; **48t** AA/Jackie Ranken; **49–50t** AA/Mike Langford; **51** AA/Jackie Ranken; **54l** AA/Jackie Ranken; **54tr** AA/Jackie Ranken; **54cr** AA/Mike Langford; **55t** AA/Mike Langford; **55cl** AA/Jackie Ranken; **55cr** AA/Jackie Ranken; **56l** AA/Jackie Ranken; **56r** AA/Jackie Ranken; **57l** Japan National Tourist Organisation/© Y. Shimizu; **57r** AA/Mike Langford; **58l** AA/Mike Langford; **58c** AA/Jackie Ranken; **58r** AA/Jackie Ranken; **59l** AA/Mike Langford; **59r** AA/Mike Langford; **60t** AA/Jackie Ranken; **60bl** AA/Mike Langford; **60br** AA/Jim Holmes; **61t** AA/Jackie Ranken; **62t** AA/Jackie Ranken; **63t** AA/Jackie Ranken; **64t** AA/Mike Langford; **65** AA/Mike Langford; **68l** AA/Mike Langford; **68tr** AA/Jackie Ranken; **68cr** AA/Mike Langford; **69t** AA/Mike Langford; **69cl** AA/Mike Langford; **69cr** AA/Jackie Ranken; **70t** AA/Mike Langford; **70c** AA/Mike Langford; **71t** AA/Jackie Ranken; **71cl** AA/Jackie Ranken; **71cr** AA/Mike Langford; **72tl** AA/Mike Langford; **72tr** AA/Mike Langford; **73l** AA/Jackie Ranken; **73r** AA/Jackie Ranken; **74cl** AA/Jackie Ranken; **74cr** AA/Mike Langford; **75cl** AA/Mike Langford; **75cr** AA/Jackie Ranken; **76t** AA/Jackie Ranken; **76bl** AA/Mike Langford; **76br** AA/Jackie Ranken; **77t** AA/Jackie Ranken; **78t** AA/Jackie Ranken; **79t** AA/Jackie Ranken; **80** AA/Mike Langford; **81–82t** AA/Mike Langford; **83** AA/Jackie Ranken; **86l** AA/Jackie Ranken; **86–87t** AA/Mike Langford; **86–87c** AA/Jackie Ranken; **87tr** AA/Jackie Ranken; **87cr** AA/Mike Langford; **88l** AA/Mike Langford; **88r** AA/Mike Langford; **89l** AA/Mike Langford; **89r** AA/Mike Langford; **90l** AA/Douglas Corrance; **90–91t** Japan National Tourist Organisation; **90cr** Peter Horree/Alamy; **91r** AA/Douglas Corrance; **91cl** Ian Leonard/Alamy; **91cr** Ian Leonard/Alamy; **92–93t** AA/Jackie Ranken; **92bl** AA/Jackie Ranken; **92br** AA/Mike Langford; **93bl** AA/Jackie Ranken; **93br** AA/Jackie Ranken; **94t** AA/Jackie Ranken; **95t** AA/Jackie Ranken; **95c** AA/Jackie Ranken; **96** AA/Mike Langford; **97** AA/Jackie Ranken; **100tl** AA/Jackie Ranken; **100cl** AA/Mike Langford; **100–101** AA/Mike Langford; **102l** AA/Jackie Ranken; **102r** AA/Jackie Ranken; **103l** © Disney Enterprises, Inc. **103r** © Disney Enterprises, Inc. **104t** AA/Jackie Ranken; **104b** AA/Mike Langford; **105** AA/Mike Langford; **106** AA/Mike Langford; **107** AA/Mike Langford; **108–112** AA/Clive Sawyer; **108(i)** AA/Mike Langford; **108(ii)** AA/Mike Langford; **108(iii)** AA/Mike Langford; **113** AA/Mike Langford; **114–125t** AA/Mike Langford; **115br** Stockbyte; **118bl** AA/Jackie Ranken; **120** MRI Bankers' Guide to Foreign Currency, Houston, USA; **121** AA/Jackie Ranken; **123** AA/Jackie Ranken; **124bl** AA/Jim Holmes; **124bc** AA/Mike Langford; **124br** AA/Mike Langford; **125bl** AA/Jackie Ranken; **125br** AA/Mike Langford

Every effort has been made to trace the copyright holders, and we apologise in advance for any unintentional omissions or errors. We would be pleased to apply any corrections in any following edition of this publication.